Dedicated to my daughters,
and all the hardy women in my life.

DON'T PANIC

A Business Guide to Small Scale

Cut Flower Farming

Sarah Adams

Table of Contents

Introduction

I'm thrilled to be able to offer an expanded edition of this book. I was truly humbled by the response to my first limited printing. Releasing a book is scary stuff! I'm so glad I've been able to help others create solid, practical plans for their growing businesses.

This book was initially written as a manual for a cut flower business course I developed after my first year of running Alberta Girl Acres. The response to both the course and the manual was so wonderfully eager, that I poured the content into a book and offered it to growers beyond my limited prairie borders. Now, after gathering more experience and perspective, I've expanded on several topics, added chapters, and delved deeper into what setting up a cut flower growing business entails.

The book is written from my perspective, as a grower in the Canadian prairies (Southern Alberta, zone 4a), and is designed to be accessible to newbies with little to no previous experience running a small business. Throughout this book, I utilize my professional background within communications and marketing, as well as my various experiences with small business development, to offer as comprehensive a guide as possible. Because this guide is about business management rather than growing, my hope is that dreamers both in Canada and beyond will enjoy it while visioning and starting their new cut flower businesses, or reassessing their existing ones.

And of course, thank you to everyone who shared their experiences or contributed their advice. I'll never grow tired of hearing or reading it!

Thank you and happy dreaming!

Left page: A summer sunset featuring our field grown larkspur.

The Dream

A flower farm. Really, what could be more dreamy?

Awakening each morning as the summer sun rises, slipping on a sundress and gliding through your gardens as the birds sing choruses around you. Balancing tea in one hand, a stylish notepad in the other, you laugh and gently chide your dog as he chases a multicoloured rabble of butterflies into the breeze. Your adorable barn cat, who would never *think* of using the peony patch as a litter box, is gently swatting one of the many ladybugs sipping the morning dew from your rows and rows of weed-free, pest-free, disease-free, 100% organic, perfectly formed long stemmed blooms.

Your loving and financially independent partner calls you from the kitchen. He baked muffins! He brings one to you while also carrying several fence posts. "When I'm finished with these, where would you like the new flower bed?" he asks. "If I know you," he chides adoringly, "you've spent another small fortune on plants you have no room for!". Blushing, you confess you have, which sets him into a gleeful uproar, "I love how it helps me collect points on my credit card!". He kisses your cheek and sets off, "I shall build a new barn for you today as well my love! For your workshops!". You sigh. You are so glad you started this farm.

Or something like that. Right?

It's pretty easy to imagine how perfect life would be as a flower farmer. And thanks to Instagram and other social media platforms, we get to scroll through a steady stream of shimmering examples, all day every day; Floret, The Flower Hat, Bluma Flower Farm, Antonio Valente... their arms loaded with perfect blooms, impeccably tended beds, smiling faces... they seem so fulfilled. So balanced. We soak up these pastoral heroes and their stories all year long.

Above: An armload of cosmos.

The Dream calls to us, combining romantic notions of living harmoniously with the cycles of nature, dedicating all our energy towards growing beautiful things that make people happy, and being our own boss. Bliss!

This may read as though it's building up to a cynical "WELL GUESS WHAT, IT'S LIES! ALL LIES!", but it's not! And it isn't! True, the morning sun will not always herald the beginning of another dreamy day. Your blooms will struggle, your pets will betray you, and your partner, if you have one, will have "PATIENCE" forcibly tattooed on their forehead. There will be days of pure slog, when the very best you can do is lay face down in the dirt and point limply at a weed. BUT...

For those obsessed with planning, planting, and growing pretty things, flower farming is still about as close as it gets to the perfect job. There will be many mornings where the light and landscape take your breath away. The days that you step into your flower beds and stare in wonder at the beauty you've cultivated will be frequent.

The intensity of well-being that comes from this life will, on occasion, be met with hardship that is equal and opposite to your bliss, but those times only make the beauty of your livelihood more radiant when it reappears.

And while flower farming is tough (really tough) and your early years will be tough (REALLY TOUGH), positioning your farm as a *business first* is imperative. Otherwise it will become a very expensive hobby which, for people with ample financial support, is lovely! But you're not here to foster an expensive hobby. You're here to start a business, and having all the business elements in place before you jump in will ensure your blissful days far outnumber the days of laying face down in the dirt pointing limply at weeds.

From here, it's important to acknowledge that EVERY new business struggles in its early years. Ask any small business owner, and they will tell you the first couple years are ROUGH. Everything is new. It's all one continuous learning curve, you barely sleep, and it's expensive.

The good news is, a start up cut flower business has many advantages over start ups in other industries!

Above: A late summer harvest of seed-grown dahlias, cosmos, and a mix of other beauties.

For one thing, our product is GORGEOUS. Can a picture of a panini compete with a picture of a dahlia? Does a person sigh and release the tension in their neck when they see a photo of socks? Does an image of a muffin remind someone of the happiest day of their life? Well, maybe. Depends on the muffin.

The point is: flowers are very good at selling themselves, because people's relationships to flowers are deep and tender. We all know this. It's why we want to spend our lives growing them.

I've had more people than I can count tell me about the flowers their mothers, fathers, or grandparents grew. The flowers they had at their wedding. The flowers that brought them peace when they lost their loved one.

And of course there's also the cultural significance of flowers. Food and clothing are essential, to be sure. But flowers, with no practical purpose other than bringing joy and comfort, are something else entirely. I can't think of a lovelier profession than ushering these beauties into the world. Flowers mean something, to so many.

Left page: Early summer storms continue to increase in intensity due to climate change. Storms are a serious risk for any grower.

The Reality

The reality of cut flower farming is that it's like any other sort of farming; long, physically demanding days during peak seasons, ongoing uncertainty due to weather and various uncontrollable conditions, and slow spells during the off season. The difference, of course, is that rather than growing armloads of carrots or squash for hungry stomachs, you're growing armloads of zinnias or cosmos for hungry hearts. Awe!

Whatever your product, in the small scale market farming game, you have to HUSTLE. Your business won't do anything for you if you can't sell your product. Are you a salesperson? You need to be. Sometimes all that means is good writing skills and being able to smile for a camera, but make no mistake, your prerogative is to make those sales. If sales don't interest you, then you'll definitely be happier as a hobby gardener, and there's no shame in that!

I started my farm as an "all in" venture. After years of waiting for the "perfect time" to live my dream... the perfect partner, the perfect income, the perfect ages of my kids... I decided life was starting to feel awfully short, and the perfect time might never come. Like having a child, there will always be a reason not to. Often several perfectly good reasons!

Not everyone wants to have a child, and not everyone wants to run a business. But when you do, you REALLY DO. You know it in your bones. It's simply a part of who you are, and whether your ambitions lie in parenthood or entrepreneurship, it just so happens that a child and a business are very similar…

In the early years, both will demand your attention at all hours. Both take exorbitant amounts of mental and physical energy. Both will make you bolt upright at 3am because THEY NEED YOU.

Both are expensive. Both will challenge your identity, your social life, your patience. Both will involve a lot of tantrums. Both can be absolute devils and dreams-come-true, simultaneously.

The bonus to a business is that it's more likely to start turning a profit around year five, and if it ends up being a bad fit, you can always sell or dissolve it ;).

Once again, I can't stress enough that this life you're dreaming of, this lovely adventure, is a *business*. Your new cut flower farm or yard is a startup. A startup business is consuming and expensive during its early years. This is not a "get rich quick" scheme, and unless you're already a very skilled gardener, the growing elements will be a challenge to master as well, on top of managing your new business.

You will be working very hard. It will be tiring and stressful. The ups and downs will be intense. Selling flowers for profit is about so much more than cheerfully delivering buckets of blooms to bright and airy florist shops.

I'm not emphasizing this to scare you, but to ground you. My first year of business was one of the hardest of my life, I stretched myself further and thinner than I ever thought I could. I sacrificed my social life, my city comforts, and my financial stability to make my dream come true. Without a doubt, what got me through was having a plan. I visioned and anticipated every conceivable element of my business, set projections, and stepped forward with a blueprint. In my first year, we met my baseline projections, grossing $25 000 on less than 1/4 acre. In my second year, we met my moderate

Above: Burgundy amaranth, shredded by hail. Right page: An unprotected dahlia after an autumn snowfall.

projections, grossing $55 000 growing on just under an acre, turning a small profit. I could not have generated a profit in year two without a plan. Moving forward, my aim is to stabilize and specialize, keeping both our input and output steady while gradually increasing profits. I still write and rewrite business plans and projections annually.

If you can mentor with someone beforehand, do it. If you can spend time on another small market farm, do it. And remember that the dreamy farms you hope to emanate one day have several seasons of trial and error under their belts. The established beds, the infrastructure, the pest and weather mitigation practices, the markets; they've developed all of those pieces over years of hard work. They've earned their rewards, and so must you.

The Reality

From those who've been there...

Mara Tyler, The Farm at Oxford

"It's ok for you to change focus. You'll try things and dislike them or maybe surprisingly love something over something else. It's ok to change the focus of your business. Maybe you started out loving annuals and realize you really want to focus elsewhere. Don't be afraid to change it up and respect it as it evolves. It's your business, you outline the parameters for yourself and define your own success.

Everyone's experiences are not your own. It is natural for us to want to read up or take courses, learning is important. However, there is nothing that replaces your own experience and trials. I always encourage people to try it yourself. One person's way to do it may not be the best for you and that's ok. It doesn't discount anyone else's knowledge to do things your own way."

Chester County, Pennsylvania, USA
@thefarmatoxford
www.thefarmatoxford.com

Sarah DeAnne Benedict

"Keep good records of when, what and where I plant. Read great books like yours that break down the details of starting a flower business. Be realistic, learn from others and keep looking for ways to grow."

Marilyn Yordy, Fox Springs Farm

"The biggest mistake I made was in doing no succession planting. I am so ready and organized this year. We shall see!"

@foxspringsfarm

From those who've been there...

Ben Cooper, Coops Blooms

"We started with expectations to grow, have fun and see what worked in year one, then expand. Well we didn't even have buyers lined up or any real game plan. Kinda went with the "grow it they will come" plan. Not a smart idea.

Bought books, searched YouTube, took local classes, did the online Floret course. Tried doing flowers, fruits, veggies, chickens, and composting worms. It was just too much and we were quickly overwhlemed.

We knew all along that we would keep our real jobs and that if we failed it would still be okay and we would grow for ourselves. If we did well, then we could figure out how to make it work.

We are going to keep trying with a better plan and see what happens."

Matthews, North Carolina, USA
@coopsblooms

Cathy McGregor Smith
McSmith's Organic Farm

"It's been a long time since our first year as organic farmers... since 1984. It was really tough in the beginning, people weren't as open to coming to the farm or farmer's market then. We tried to diversify as much as possible, but after so many years we believe the best trait is "stick-to-it-ness". Now our daughter is a flower farmer! (Harris Flower Farm @harrisflowerfarm)

St Thomas, Ontario, Canada
@mcsmithorganicfarm

Kalli Pigot, Dancing Dandelion Farms

I think the best thing we did in our first year was to have a farm mentor with about eight 1 hour meetings prior to the growing season. We did this through the Young Agragarians (a Canadian grassroots initiative). I can't imagine what it would have been like without our mentor. Mainly he built up our confidence and assured us our crop plan looked reasonable. He also helped us make a business plan.

@dancing_dandelion_farms
Duncan, BC, Canada

From those who've been there...

Megan McGuire Beauman, Red Daisy Farm

"I accidentally became a flower farmer! I've always loved to grow veggies, and when we moved to our small, 4 acre farm, I was so excited to grow big, beautiful gardens. My first year was a complete flop! Everything I tried to grow just failed. I couldn't understand it, I was always a successful gardener. We finally had our water tested, and it came back as "not suitable for irrigation"! The sodium in our water was so high, it was killing the root systems of every plant we put in the ground. I was devastated. We researched for over a year and finally found a Zetacore, which basically neutralizes sodium in the water.

Fast forward a year, and my cousin got engaged and asked me if she could have her wedding at our farm! I said "sure, and I'll even grow all of your wedding flowers!" I still didn't really know the first thing about growing flowers, but I stayed up late every night googling "how to grow flowers" lol. With a lot of note taking, we created growing beds, laid netafim irrigation, and once May rolled around we put the seeds and bulbs in the ground and went on a wing and a prayer!

Long story short, the flowers were beautiful and perfect for her wedding! I was officially bit by the flower farming bug! We now farm on 3/4 acre, and we are grossing close to $100k on flower sales, mostly wholesale, and direct to florists. I look forward to every new season, and love to see how far we've come in just five years!

Do what you love, work hard, and never give up on your dreams! You'll know in your heart if this gig is for you after year one, you just will! "

Brighton, Colorado, USA
@reddaisyfarm

Shannon J, Broadfork Farm

"Our biggest challenge in the first year with cut flowers as an add-on enterprise (to vegetables) was marketing. We were the only ones at our farmer's market selling cut flowers, and customers weren't used to seeing/buying farm fresh flowers. Cut flowers have become our fastest growing enterprise in sales, though marketing/selling is still our biggest bottleneck."

River Hebert, Nova Scotia, Canada
@broadforkfarmers

From those who've been there...

Heather Griffiths, Wasatch Blooms

"I wrote a five year goal plan, and in my first year achieved all of my first year goals, some of my second year, and one of my third year goals. I would say making a five year goal plan was essential for me. I learned what I did not want to do, and who my ideal customer was. Making the plan helped me know what to say no to. I am focusing on slow consistent growth, mastering the first skill before I move onto the next, saying no to some opportunities so I can take on the opportunities that speak to me. If there was one thing that made my first year work for me, it was knowing that I didn't have to do everything all in my that year, because I had it written for the next year or the year after. I know what my long term goals are and I am taking the steps to get there."

Salt Lake City, Utah, USA
@wasatchblooms

Maria Michelle Panter, Save the Bees Flower Co.

"Investing in myself was a big hurdle for me, and if I had realized how big of an investment it really was... I may not have had the courage. Once I was neck deep though, there was no going back. My goals are to up my seed starting game by switching to soil blocking and homemade seed staing mix. Plus, registering my side hustle and keeping all my business finances separate from my personal finances. I always tell other newbies to read read read, and get their resale tax number asap so they can take advantage of wholesale prices right away."

Wasatch Front, Utah, USA
@savethebeesflowerco

Left page: Even one acre can seem overwhelming to a single grower. It takes a lot of planning and hard work to convert a field of grass and weeds into flowers.

The Plan

A business plan is important for several reasons: for one, it's a road map and reference for the times when you're so lost in the grind you can't remember your own name, let alone who you're supposed to be marketing to. It's also a crucial tool if you're entering into a partnership; both parties should develop and agree on the plan before entering into a formal commitment. And if you're seeking funding such as business loans, banks and lending groups will want to see a fully formed plan before lending startup funds.

Think of your first year in business as your "foundation year", similar to a first year of university. Stay flexible and open to different ideas and opportunities, and eventually you'll land on a "major" and a few "minors", ie: products and markets that work best for you.

While there are plenty of business plan templates available online, your business plan will be as unique as your business is. Templates are handy in terms of understanding formatting, but there is no "fill in the blank" plan that will result in a cohesive, or even helpful, map of your new business. A business plan takes time to develop. Each chapter in this book will dig into the various pieces your business plan should include, such as branding and key messaging, communications, HR, production, identifying markets, marketing, operations, etc.

A final, fully formed plan often takes months to complete, so don't feel intimidated or overwhelmed if you can't identify and sort all the information we discuss in this book right away. It will feel like a lot, but have patience.

And of course, your plan doesn't have to be set in stone. It can and will change from year to year. Maybe you'll want to go full wholesale in year three, or maybe you'll decide to add an event venue in year five. Expansion, downsizing, altered courses, new crops, accidental success in unexpected markets... as a business owner, these are all exciting paths you get to navigate!

Above: Summer sunflowers and chocolate laceflower (Ammi Dara).

In small business, the room for innovation and experimentation is vast, limited only by permits, licensing and cash flow. With a comprehensive plan in place from the get-go, you can more easily see the bigger picture as your business shifts from year to year. You might actually cycle through two or three different business ideas as you step into this venture, depending on how new the whole enterprise is to you, and how adaptable you are to opportunity. Which brings us to a key point: no matter how new or experienced you are as a business owner, ADAPTABILITY is the primary trait you will require to succeed.

Before I bought my farm, I was still in the midst of researching sustainable rural livelihoods, and the first draft of my business plan was actually focused on garlic and eggs! After learning about New Oxley Garlic and Forage & Farm, two exceptional garlic farms in Southern Alberta, I felt that maybe the local garlic market was covered well enough. And when I worked out the financial projections for selling fresh farm eggs, the profits were just too small, with far too high an overhead. Then I wrote another draft that included sour cherries and liqueurs, which was quickly nixed due to the time it would take for the cherry trees to mature and the AGLC's (Alberta Gaming, Liquor and Cannabis) strict regulations (I still planted twenty cherry trees when I bought my farm though, just in case!). At the same time, I had been reading up on cut flower production, and as every other plan fell to the wayside (perennial herbs, lavender, sheep's wool), the case for cut flowers became stronger and stronger.

As I read and re-read Jean-Martin Fortier's The Market Gardener, Eliot Coleman's The New Organic Grower, and M.G. Kains' Five Acres and Independence, I was beginning to circle in on a more solid and sustainable plan. Finally, I discovered Floret Farm's Cut Flower Garden, and the deal was sealed.

Below: A cheerful seed-grown dahlia in the field.

Not only was the entire prospect of growing cut flowers for a living just the dreamiest, but my marketing background was jumping up and down yelling "YES YES YES", both because of how easy flowers are to present and photograph (ie: market), and also because the local cut flower game in my region had barely begun.

And while other start ups often have to contend with competition, cut flower growing is an industry that actually gets *better* and *easier* the more there are doing it! Growers can coordinate, commiserate, and lean on each while learning and growing. Together they are able to serve the local market more effectively while also covering each others' backs in the event of freaks frosts, mini plagues, anarchist deer, hail from hell, and an endless list of other, equally delightful maelstroms.

In many places, the local flower movement is just starting to emerge! There is a HUGE market with TONS of opportunities and potential for cut flower businesses of all sizes.

And if you're growing in an area where other growers are already established, you have the advantage of networking opportunities, potential mentors, and a wealth of expertise to learn from. Wherever you're starting from, you've already got a leg up!

VISIONING

Before delving into the nitty gritties of your business, it's important to vision the scale and ambitions of your enterprise. Do you want a tidy little operation, supplying two or three florists within a limited growing season? Maybe you just want to start with a farmer's market and see how it goes. Or maybe you want to revolutionize your local flower industry, growing acres and acres of sustainable local blooms.

Breaking down what the core drive of your business is, and then assessing all you want to achieve within it, will help hone your plan and vision, create long term strategies for flexibility and growth, and will build a solid scaffolding for surviving your early years.

We're going to try a method of visioning that I hope will help you determine exactly what sort of enterprise you're about to jump into. We're going to create a "Mind Map". It's a "several drafts" process, and there is ZERO pressure to get it right on the first try. Here's how it works:

Write "CUT FLOWER BUSINESS" at the top of a large page or whiteboard. Now simply brainstorm every other word related to your CUT FLOWER BUSINESS, and add it to the page or board. From each word, you may be inspired to add more words that expound on the concept; in that case add those words closer to the "parent" word.

If you bounce to a different stream of thought, find a new area to add those words. Most importantly, let loose and pile in every word. Add more sheets if you need to, or bring in another whiteboard if you happen to have one kicking around (because who doesn't! Lol).

Here are "prompt" words you can add if you're stuck: BALANCE, MARKET, SCALE, FARM, RISK, BUDGET, SEASONAL.

From a word such as BALANCE, you might add TIME, CAPACITY, FAMILY, FINANCES, FITNESS… etc. Now, around each of those words, add more that expound on that idea.

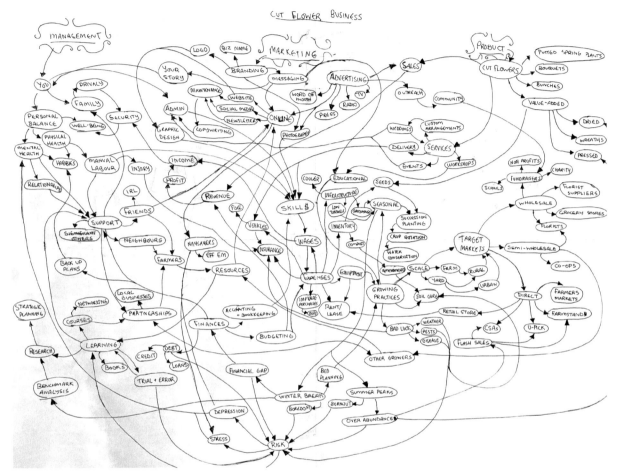

Above: One of the many drafts of my original Mind Map.

From a word such as MARKET, you might add FARMER'S MARKETS, FARM STAND, FLORIST, WHOLESALE, BRIDES, U-PICK, CSAs... etc. From here, you'll naturally be led to words such as LABOUR. which ties to CAPACITY and WAGES, which ties to FINANCES. Or FAMILY (which ties to LABOUR), which leads to SUPPORT, which ties to BALANCE.

Circle each word on the page, and start connecting them with lines and arrows. When one word "leads" to another, indicate the progression with a little arrow. This process will get messy, and you'll soon find arrows and lines are criss-crossing all over the page. Let it happen!

25

Once you've connected all the ideas, take note of the emerging themes and concepts. You may find there are several ideas related to "Business Management", "Personal Needs", or "Product". Make note of those themes for your next draft.

This map is much like your brain when starting a new business: messy, jumbled, bursting with a million ideas and concerns. While overwhelming, it's SO important to lay them all out where you can really see and address them. Ignoring them will not make them go away, and will only add to your newbie anxiety.

Now take the prominent themes from your first (or second) draft, and transfer them over to a fresh page or board. Add the related words you brainstormed in your previous drafts, circling them again and mapping them according to their relevance and importance.

You may find yourself reworking the map again and again, moving words towards more orderly clusters, consolidating several words into one concept, and deleting words that don't fit anymore. Some words may take on greater significance than expected. You might suddenly see several arrows pointing to one word... that one word is probably a key concept of your business! Feel free to colour code words too; maybe colour "short term" words green, and "long term" words yellow...

You might look at your reworked draft and see another mess. That's okay! In fact, the more times you rework your map, the more comprehensive it will become, and the more it will reveal exactly what you want from your business.

When completed, this map will become your mental keystone while working through your business plan. You'll see prioritized themes that will help you identify where you'll need to focus in your first year. As I went through the process, I reworked my map about ten times, and the words that ultimately stood out were "SUPPORT", "ONLINE", "RISK", and "SKILL$" (ie: saleable skills). And in my first year, those were exactly the areas where I spent most of my energy.

Your mind map will be unique to your vision, strengths, and limitations. It will help you strategize your short and long term goals throughout your early years, and will remind you that every aspect of your business is interrelated, one almost always affecting the other.

Did you find creating the mind map challenging? Stressful? Frustrating? Tedious? Overwhelming? Good.

Your business, while fuelled by your dreamiest and most idyllic ambitions, is also a beast. Facing the beast head on from the start will prevent surprise attacks, helping you handle and tame it as time passes. Eventually, with patience and learning, it will be everything you imagined and more.

Above: There are many ways to be prepared for risks beyond your control. Always plan for the worst and hope for the best!

RISK & MITIGATION

An important theme that will likely arise in your mind map is "RISK". It's impossible to start a risk-free business. And in the cut flower business, the risks greet you each morning as you face your self-made venture, which might also happen to be your front yard. "Hello!" calls the tiny army of thrips. "Mornin!" wave the dark storm clouds on the horizon. "What's up?" chirps your phone, filling with queries and reminders faster than you can answer them.

Hail. Burnout. Pests. Financial strain. Drought. Debt. Mechanical failure. Injury. Frost. Weeds. Illness. Depression. Overabundance. Empty markets. It's easy to tuck these bummers out of sight when planning your dreamscape, but they'll find you! It's your job to be ready for them, in whatever way you can be.

In this world, our very best friend is the word "MITIGATION".

Mitigation strategies will involve research, support systems, and adaptability. You will need to call upon all of your innermost strength, patience, logic, and cool headedness, and you'll need to get very good at using those abilities to rework your well-laid, exhaustively considered plans *on a dime*. Sometimes nixing them altogether!

In the following pages, let's review some common cut flower farming risks, and address some mitigation strategies for each:

27

Risk 1: Crop Failure

You did everything right, yet here you are. A hailstorm, a swarm of grasshoppers, drought, floods, thrips, fungus, rust, herbicidal drift, an overeager husband with a lawnmower… whatever happened, it's devastating. You shake your fists at the heavens, wail into the void (or at the husband), then grab a drink and pour one out in the garden, for all that could have been. In your early years, with your hopes SO high and your experience SO low, it's easy to see crop failure as The End.

But listen, we've all been there. We've cried. We've thrown tantrums. We've run into gale force winds yelling "NO NO NO NO NO" as our low tunnels sailed gracefully through our neighbour's yard. There's no fool-proof version of farming. We're fools aplenty out here.

There are many, many options when it comes to mitigating crop failure, but the one I most strongly advocate for, is this: in your first couple years, make as few promises as possible. Are you growing Cafe au Lait dahlias? Lovely. Don't promise them to a soul. Do you expect a bumper crop of sunflowers? Great! Sell them when you have them, not before. Find a way to move your flowers with as little commitment to any specific crop as possible, ie: weekly bunches at a farmer's market, mixed bouquet CSAs during peak season, or an adventurous florist. Doing so will mitigate the ripple effect of disappointment when any crops are lost. Nothing is worse than losing your

pretties, mourning them, and then peeving off expectant customers because something you had no control over wiped out your beauties.

Otherwise, ensuring healthy crops begins with research and healthy soil. Google any pest or threat along with the words "mitigation" or "control", and you will find dozens of techniques and options. Speak to other gardeners to identify the top threats you might be dealing with in your area, and prioritize addressing those threats long before you've planted a single seed in the ground.

For myself, growing in the Southern Alberta prairies, my top crop risks are:

DROUGHT: Mitigated via drip irrigation, rain water harvesting, and utilizing our clay-heavy soil for moisture retention. I also leave plants in beds over the winter to catch and accumulate snow, and cover any unused beds with cover crops or seasonal, permeable landscape fabric. In the summer, I try to companion plant ground cover with taller plants, ie: nasturtiums with sunflowers, clover with corn, etc.

WIND: Mitigated via heavy duty steel structures with reinforced anchors. I also strategically plant the field using sturdy tall plants as windbreaks (ie: ammi dara, amaranth, sunflowers, grasses, cosmos), and we are slowly establishing permanent natural wind breaks. EVERYTHING must be weighted, deeply stapled, or tied down, including landscape fabric, trellises, and mulch.

DEER: Mitigated via a basic t-post and fishing line "deer fence" (google it!) around the perimeter of the field, paired with solar powered predator lights. So far this method works wonderfully for us.

THRIPS: Mitigated via diatomaceous earth sprinkled liberally over the soil starting in May, and then bi-weekly (twice a month) throughout the growing season. Well amended soil keeps plants healthier and less vulnerable to infestations as well.

APHIDS: Mitigated via live ladybugs and green lacewing, as well as neem oil and diluted milk sprays. I also hand squash colonies as I see them. We will also be implementing more control over nearby ant colonies, as the ants farm aphids and increase their numbers. In the later season when the plants are fully mature, we also let our chickens roam. They make wonderful pest hunters.

TARNISHED PLANT BUGS: Mitigated via neem and garlic sprays, trap crops such as alfalfa, and protective organza bags over blooms.

POWDERY MILDEW: Mitigated via airflow and soured skim milk spray.

HAIL: Mitigated via planting "hail resilient" flowers, ie: flowers that do well with pinching. We also grow many flowers inside a high

Above: A moment of reflection in our early summer field.

tunnel, and we are establishing hail screens over many of our field beds.

WEEDS: Weeds sure love life! As irritating overachievers, they can sometimes be harvested and used, but in many other cases, they are noxious and will choke out your pretties if given the chance. We mitigate weeds via low till/no till methods (every time you till, you bring thousands more weed seeds to the surface!), cover crops, landscape fabric, and good old fashioned hand pulling. Weeding is a full time job during the growing season, and to keep our insects, soil and surrounding ecosystems healthy, we avoid using herbicides.

Risk 2: Debt

Perhaps one of the most formidable risks, and the one that prevents many would-be market farmers from jumping in, is debt. Start up costs for a market farm are not cheap, and depending on your scale and resources, initial expenses could be anywhere from $5000 to $100k. If you're seeking funding from a bank or lending group, the risk becomes all the more potent. You could potentially be carrying new debt equal to a small mortgage. Is it worth it?

It is, if you have a plan. Without one, you can't accurately assess what you'll need, in terms of start up equipment and supplies, to get your business off the ground. You also can't qualify for any loan funding without a solid business plan and projections. There are some grants available, but many require at least two years of business tax returns to qualify.

Your plan will clarify and prioritize what your NEEDS are versus your WANTS. It doesn't take much to grow 1/4 acre of flowers. It's essentially just a big garden! BUT: how many months do you want to have flowers for… will you need season extenders? How soon after harvest will your flowers be sold… will you need a walk in cooler? How will you be transporting your flowers…will you need a vehicle? What are you willing to invest in marketing your flowers… will you need a new camera? Who will be doing all the labour…will you need a seasonal employee?

You don't need EVERYTHING right away to get started, but depending on your early goals, certain pieces will be critical to ensuring a successful start. If, after all your planning and careful consideration, your plan shows that you need $50k in start up capital, securing that capital is most likely to happen via new debt. For many of us, that option is simply unavoidable.

In my first year, I prioritized a BCS walk behind tractor, a diy walk-in cooler (built inside a secure outbuilding), and a 100' x 25' unheated greenhouse. For my business to reach my goal of turning a profit by year two, I decided these were the key elements it would require from the start. For that reason, I sought startup funding.

I secured my start up loan through a Canadian non-profit group called Community Futures. Their mandate is to build small rural businesses and support rural entrepreneurs. While the application process was rigorous, the biggest advantage to working with them, as opposed to a bank, was that their teams are made up of compassionate humans who have advised me through the various ups and downs of my start up journey. They care about, and are invested in, seeing my business succeed. In that regard, the debt feels much easier to carry.

Risk 3: Injury

The most precious tool you'll ever use on your farm is your body, and when you're just starting out, it's likely you'll be doing most of the hard labour yourself. If your body breaks, your fledgling enterprise could screech to a halt as well. And if you have others helping on the farm, protecting yourself and your business from liability is critical.

Understanding your tools and equipment, researching safety protocols, and ensuring everyone on the farm is trained and capable, is the first step to mitigating injury. The second is insurance, which we cover more in "Human Relations" (p.169).

It's also extremely important to keep your body as able as possible. Stretch and strengthen throughout the year, not just during the growing season. Reinforce weak joints with braces, see a doctor if something feels off, and always ask for help if something is beyond your physical scope. Wear sun protection and hydrate well in the heat. On especially hot days, we start extra early and take an afternoon "siesta" (which, for me, includes emails and computer work). Pacing and awareness of your physical capacity, as well as keeping an eye on those around you, will go a long way towards keeping your operation sustainable.

Risk 4: Burnout

In a perfect world, we can do it all. Everyone else seems to be doing it, right? A new business is extremely exciting, and when you see your skills and passion pay off, it's a wonderful rush! Your first seasons of flowers will amaze you. You'll take daily delight in all the new colours, smells, routines, connections, and developments. As your business plan unfolds, it's a whirlwind of learning and progress. You'll feel energized, alive, inspired, and then... wham. You will hit a wall.

We all do. Especially when taking on a massive new project. I call it "post achievement depression", and while it can strike anyone, anywhere, it usually strikes at specific times. A massive project consumes all our energy as we roll out plans, run with ideas, and delight in seeing our creations take shape. Conditioned by the constant adrenaline and action, when it's suddenly cut off, we go through an intense cycle of withdrawal. Suddenly, we feel aimless, dangling over an emotional chasm of "what now".

For me, this hits in the early fall, after the frost has halted flower production and the freight train of "SUMMER BOUNTY" has skidded to a sudden halt. It doesn't matter that I know, every year, the seasons will change. It doesn't matter whether I had a great year or a hard one. Every fall, all of the tension and

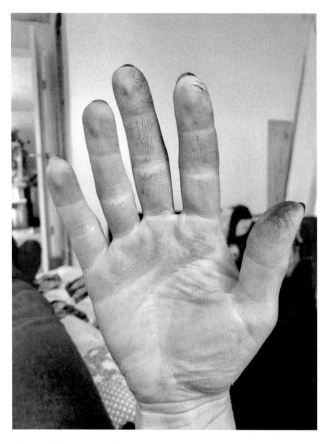

Above: This was as clean as I could get my hands at the peak of our season. Stains and cracks from harvests are common, and I found myself saying "they're clean! I promise!" a lot.

expectations of our whirlwind season unravel precariously in my body and my brain. The sudden shift in routine, coupled with seeing all my beautiful blooms go from dazzling to dead… it's a total mind job. It's when I'm most vulnerable to burn out, and when I lean heavily on my support network.

Which brings us to mitigating burn out: Support. You'll need support. You'll need someone, either family or friends, to sooth and comfort you when the weight suddenly feels too heavy. You'll need someone who understands how hard you've worked, how much you've earned your downtime and rest, and how tender you will be as you recover from the season. If possible, you might need someone to tend the farm as you cocoon yourself for a week, visit friends, or just tread gently for a bit.

If you can, plan for a week of "shutting down" after your fall frost date. Find someone to cover the farm, or even just your Inbox, and give yourself that time to unravel, process, and switch seasonal gears. This is called "strategic self care". You will hit that wall, but you can prevent it from letting you sink completely. It's okay to feel overwhelmed and sad, even if everything is going great! You're a human being, not a robot. Anticipate those overwhelming emotions, surround yourself with people who can help, implement self-soothing and self-care techniques, and strategize your way through it.

Above: Our freshly tilled field, spring 2019.

Those are only a few of the risks you might face stepping into a new cut flower business. Take some time to identify all of your fears and anxieties going into this venture, then work backwards to address how you can mitigate each of those risks. The solution to almost every problem can be found somewhere either in research, support networks, or plain old trial and error.

Which brings us to an important point: **ERROR**. You're going to make mistakes. A lot of them. You can't completely mitigate every problem. You can't plan and research away every bump in the road. Mitigation isn't about eliminating risk entirely, it's about being prepared for it. Even if it just means having a shoulder to cry on (or several shoulders to cry on), the point of creating mitigation strategies is to ensure the bad luck and annoying blips are as fast and painless as possible, so you can LEARN, then bounce back into the game.

During one of our business course sessions, a participant brought up another risk I'd never considered: **noncommittment**. It actually took me a moment to let the concept to sink in, because "commitment" was never optional for me. My farm was always "all in"; flower farming is my full-time job, my main source of income, and it consumes almost every moment of my life. I make big jumps and put myself "out there" because the way I see it, if I want my business to thrive, and if I want to support my family, there's simply no other choice but to fully commit.

But for others thinking growing flowers might be a nice replacement for their 9-5 jobs, or for those who have secondary income to rely on, it's much harder to justify those risky jumps. It becomes easier to blur out the stressful bits and just focus on the fun stuff. Designing, growing, posting pretty photos… the glamorous bits are a lot of fun, until you realize how much that fun is costing you. When faced

Above: Kendra and our woofers, the very first month of our first growing season.

with crunching back through a year or two of neglected paperwork or surprisingly dismal returns, the go-to response might be "maybe this isn't for me". Hence, a business dies.

You *must* be prepared to face the sticky bits of your business. Make a plan that includes handling those elements. If you hate bookkeeping, find a bookkeeper! If you're hopeless on the internet, ask for help! Every gear needs to turn in order for the machine to run as a whole.

Are you nervous yet? Nerves are good! One tip I received when I used to perform, was to combat stage nerves by saying "I'm excited" rather than "I'm nervous". All your fear can be transformed by saying that simple phrase out loud. "I'm excited!"

And you should be!

At the end of my farm's first season, my wonderful farm hand, Kendra, and I were saying our goodbyes, reminiscing back to the first few days of early spring on the farm.

We couldn't believe how much we had accomplished in what felt like months of chaos. Kendra recounted how her first day of work set the tone for the coming season; I had to leave the farm for a few hours, and there was a large pile of metal greenhouse pieces that needed to be moved. It was the first task I could think of that would keep her busy until I got back, and at that point, I'd already been hauling heavy things around the farm for a few months, so I didn't even think of it as doable or not doable task, it simply needed to be done. I showed her the pile, showed her where they needed to be moved, and then zipped away on my errand.

As we remembered that day, Kendra told me she looked at the pile and thought "there's no way I can move that." But, because she had signed up for the full farm experience, and wanted to make a good impression on her first day, she got to work. By the time I returned home, the pile was moved and neatly stacked where I'd shown her.

Kendra later told me that was the day her perspective changed from "I'm not sure I can do that" to "I can do anything". That one day of facing a small mountain and championing it set the stage for the rest of her summer.

I'm so glad she told me her side of that experience. It drives home the lesson that the earlier you face those mountains and beasts, the sooner they'll feel manageable, even minimal. Put simply, there's nothing to it but to do it.

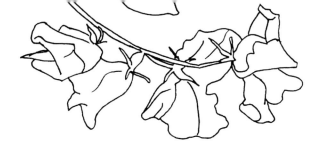

REWARD

Reward presents itself in so many ways during your early years, but sometimes it takes a keen eye to see it, or someone else's keen eyes! Empowerment and self discovery are just the beginning.

For me, my first reward was stepping out into my fields the day I took possession of my farm. Prior to purchasing the farm, I'd been renting in the city, hopping between gigs, working office jobs, single parenting, and generally feeling strung out by city life.

That day, the prairies were quiet aside from the birds, in full symphonic form. I just kept looking around at my new farm thinking "this is *mine*". It was MY space, MY dream, MY small paradise to design and build. That feeling of long awaited independence washed over me as I stood in my fields, and to this day I still wander out to that same spot when I need a breather.

Claiming your own destiny offers incredible personal rewards, even if it means hustling your buns to make it work. At least you're hustling your buns for YOU, not some faceless company or cause. I've never looked back. Five stars, highly recommended!

Aside from personal fulfillment, your cut flower business will offer several other, more tangible rewards. Profits will come eventually, and in the meantime, the floriculture industry is filled with so many amazing, supportive, and generous new friends. It is a remarkably gentle network of professionals, perhaps due to the harsher nature of farming. Everyone is eager to share their experience and knowledge (when they have time!). Like every industry, there will be the occasional buffoon or crusty grump, but for the most part, this is a safe and supportive realm of growers and farmers.

Open yourself up to new experiences, new friends, and the great unknown. Keep "FUN" at the forefront of your mind as you move through your wild early seasons, as hard as those initial challenges may feel. As long as you're truly putting your best foot forward, wonderful opportunities will come. I promise you.

COMPETITION VS. COMMUNITY

While I was developing my business plan, "competition" seemed like a valid risk. I was pushed by funders to justify all the advantages I'd have over "the competition", which is pretty standard for new small businesses. The world of business can be absolutely cut throat, which we see throughout our cities and town centres. Independent shops live and die faster than most of us can keep track; one day they're there, the next the windows have been papered and the space is up for lease.

Many people entering small business go in with the mindset of "eat or be eaten", and launch their ventures touting all the advantages they have over the competition. "FIRST", "ONLY", "BEST"... these are flags that new businesses often fly.

I come from a very community-focused scene, having worked for non-profit arts groups in Calgary for almost 15 years. The idea of competing against another small business...

people working just as hard, trying to offer a local product, with just as many stakes in the game... it just doesn't sit well with me. We need **more** local products and services. We need thriving local economies that build community, free from the clutches of cut throat Big Capitalism.

Not every industry can accommodate this position, but as we charged forward into our first season, I started to realize how much easier the business of cut flowers would actually be if there were more growers nearby to collaborate and coordinate with. It dawned on me that this is one of the few industries where it would actually get easier if more were doing it. More shared knowledge, more potential for serving the market effectively, and more risk mitigation.

For example, you might find yourself selling blooms at a farmer's market, only to see another vendor selling flowers too. The first time this happens, it will feel like a gut punch. I've been there! In this situation, you have two options: 1) You can sit sourly and let the negative feelings and insecurity consume you (putting off potential customers with your weird vibes. Trust me, people can feel you!), or, 2) You can GET BACK TO WORK, slap on a smile, and keep chatting with your potential customers.

Heck, go over and talk to the other vendor! Drop your competitive angst and introduce yourself. Compliment their flowers. Ask where they grow them, do they offer other floral services? Is there potential for collaboration between the two of you? Give them your info. This person is doing what you're doing, they GET it. They could be your new best friend! Just break the ice, you'll both feel better for it.

And I can't tell you how many times customers bought flowers from one vendor, then came over to my spot and bought my flowers too. Competition can be overcome as long as you're offering the best product you can, and presenting yourself with passion and positivity. Even if your blooms are more expensive than other vendors', good customers, the ones you WANT, will be curious why. Tell them your story. Tell them your flowers' stories ("we thought we lost these to the hail but they came back, yay!"). Point out your favourites. Hype your CSAs, workshops, or design services. Charm them with an earnest love of what you do, and the sales will come. If someone pooh-poohs at your offerings, did you really want a rude and entitled customer anyway? They aren't for you. Next!

In my second year, I set up a multi-grower cut flower market. The primary aim of this market was to establish a community of local cut flower growers and consolidate our efforts in marketing and selling our blooms. The market's first year was not perfect (our location was a bust), and going forward there are many things we'll do differently, but the biggest success was that the market brought ten new growers together, where previously, I had no idea whether there was anyone else in my area growing flowers. Once we let our retail location go, we took turns working the shared flower trailer. One grower would take it to their town for a week, another grower would take it to a festival, another to their local farmer's market. By setting up a shared "market" we shared risk and consolidated efforts, while also establishing inventory processes and pricing systems. The kicker? We were able to provide a wider variety of gorgeous blooms to the public. Going forward, we now have a more cohesive idea of how several local growers can work together, to the benefit of our region's local cut flower lovers.

All that to say, while you create your business plan, keep in mind that traditional business advisors you encounter throughout the process may push you into the old school of business thinking: cut the competition! To which I would add: cut the competition… by not competing! Collaborate, reach out, establish relationships. You'll go so much further.

Our 2019 "Mini Growing Workshop", where I spent an afternoon discussing our growing methods, as well as which plants performed well for us.

Left: A custom stamp saves all the costs and waste associated with stickers. I stamp envelopes, bouquet sleeves, seed packets... it constantly comes in handy, and it was a one time expense!

Branding & Key Messaging

Your brand is the most magical and important piece when it comes to presenting your business publicly. This is the part of the planning process where all your dreams swirl together until they crystallize into solid visual and literal representations of your business.

"Branding" includes your logo and a set of associations related to your Key Messaging. It can also include your messaging style (ie: recurring salutations, signature sign offs, a unique font used in all your copywriting), a specific colour palette, a certain style of photography, or other visual or stylistic cues unique to your business. The most important element to your branding is that it stays consistent throughout your messaging, unless you decide to rebrand, which is absolutely okay if you have a basic strategy to go along with it!

CHOOSING A BUSINESS NAME

Business names can be very personal, and they often reflect YOU as much as your business.

The first tip I can offer is: try to avoid choosing a name that is the same or similar to an existing business. Not only will it annoy the heck out of the existing business, but it will muddle your marketing and confuse your customers. And besides, you want to stand out, right? You want your business to reflect YOUR unique dreams, and represent YOUR exceptional vision!

This is another point where a mind map comes in very handy. Try writing down every word that is relevant to your business identity, or go back and look at your original mind map. Identify all

41

the words that speak to the core essence of your business. You want a name that honestly encapsulates the nature of your venture.

A few more tips for your consideration:

Are you urban or rural? Farm, acreage, or backyard? Note: a farm can exist in a backyard, and the idea of a tiny city farm is very appealing to the urban market!

What are the geographical elements of your location? Foothills? Flats? Prairies? Hills? Forest? Mountains? Lakeside? Coulees? Valley?

Are there any weather-related phenomena that are common to your farm? Wind? Fog? Sunshine? Big skies?

Are there any historical family associations you want to tie into your business name? Maybe your family already owns or owned a farm, do you want to tie into that history, or branch out to create something new? Is your farm a tribute to a grandparent or relative?

Do you use another language in your family? What does the word "flower" translate to for you? Pulling your heritage into your business is another wonderful way to pay homage to your family and your story. (Blume Haus? Flor Campo?)

Are there more personal elements you'd like to include? Your name? Your gender?

And of course, your product. Some business advisors would say it's important to include some version of "flowers" in your business name, for marketing clarity. If you choose to include your product in your business title, there are a few different words to play with when it comes to "flowers". For example:

BLOOM, BLOSSOM, BUD, FLORET (that one is obviously taken), FLOWERET, POMPON, POSIES, SPRAY, PICK

And there's also GARDEN, and all its variables: BEDS, FIELDS, GREENHOUSE (or Flowerhouse?), OASIS, PATCH

Once you've written all these words down, begin circling, connecting, and playing with them. Alternately, you can write the words on separate little pieces of paper and move them around, like those cute fridge poetry magnets. "Big Sky Blooms" sounds pretty nice, right? "Maggie's Flower Field" is lovely too. One word names can carry a lot of impact too, ie: BLOOM. And it doesn't have to be catchy, punny, or particularly clever. Just make it honest! There are so many options, have fun with it!

For myself, "Alberta Girl Acres" was a personal choice. Born in Edmonton and raised in Cold Lake, I've lived in Lethbridge, Medicine Hat, Calgary, and now, Vulcan County. All towns and cities in Alberta, Canada. Years before buying my farm, I wrote a song called "Alberta Girl" that channeled my feelings about my lovely home province. "Highways lined with roses, blue skies filled with diamonds and

Above: I use our prairie landscape as often as possible in our farm's photos. It's an important piece of our branding.

cotton candy", I've spent a large portion of my life driving along Alberta roads and highways, taking in its various landscapes. It's my home and refuge, and I absolutely adore it. I'm also proud to be an independent woman making my own way, so when I finally bought my small parcel of 5.5 acres, "Alberta Girl Acres" made perfect sense.

Strategically, I also chose to leave "flowers" out of my business name, because I wanted to leave some flexibility for future growth. I will always grow flowers, but if lavender or cherries happen to do exceptionally well on my farm, I want the freedom to potentially lean towards them in my future marketing. My "brand" is Alberta Girl Acres, which can easily act as an umbrella to other products and services.

Whatever name you choose, it should make you happy, and reflect your vision and personality. This is YOUR business. Your baby! You do you!

"What if I want to change my business name?"

That's completely fine! If your business is already on social media under a certain handle, just give your followers a heads up a week or two before the switch, letting them know you'll be rebranding. Show them your new logo if you have one, explain why you decided to change it, and message that you're pumped about the change! If you have a website, make the news of your rebrand clear on your home page. After the switch, continue to message the change for a week or so afterwards, just to remind folks "Hey it's still us! Same great

43

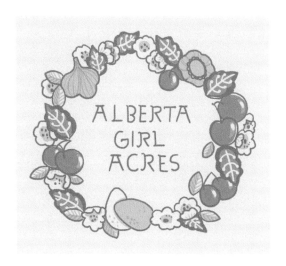

Above: Some early versions of the Alberta Girl Acres logo, designed by illustrator and tattoo artist Kiarra Albina.

flowers, new name/logo!"

YOUR LOGO

Your logo is another essential piece of your business that is deeply personal, and is a way to express a little piece of YOU to your public. While there are plenty of tips out there re: designing effective logos (ie: not too busy, legible from a distance, balanced colour and ratios…), at the end of the day it should really just be something you find beautiful and true to your vision.

Many people don't know where to start when it comes to designing a logo. If you're not artistically inclined, or don't have a background in design, I'd strongly recommend finding a professional artist, illustrator, or designer.

Not sure where to look for such talent? Start local. This is where hashtags and social media come in very handy! Search hashtags like #calgary (or your closest town/city) along with #illustrator #illustration #logodesign #design #artist, or even #tattoo. Many tattoo artists started in illustration and fine art, and the nature of tattoo sizing and line work actually translates really well into logo design (ie: the woman who did the Alberta Girl Acres logo, Kiarra Albina, is an incredible Calgary artist who started in fine art, then moved to illustration, and now does beautiful tattoo work).

Expect to pay between $1000 and $3000 for a unique, professionally designed logo. Artists need to be paid fairly for their services, and designing a logo is an involved and time

44

consuming process.

Most designers will ask for your colour palettes and any other inspirational elements you can offer, including your key messaging. It helps to have all these pieces prepped before you reach out to an artist.

Elements you should include in your request are:

- Other logos you love
- Your colour palette
- Different versions you'll need, ie: black and white, colour with outlines, colour with no outlines, vectorized files (.AI or .EPS), as well as .jpg and .png files. If you're not familiar with photoshop or image conversion software, having various file versions of your logo will save you plenty of headaches later on, and will allow for tweaks to the design in the future.
- Your key messages
- Your business name - do you want it integrated into your logo, or kept separate?
- What will you be using this logo for? Website, signage, stickers, stamps, marketing materials…?

Finding an artist who can translate your vision into a gorgeous logo isn't hard! It begins with a bit of searching, and then when you see a style that speaks to you, simply send them a message! Once they indicate they're available and willing, email them your detailed request. They should respond with a price quote, and may clarify their process, ie: three different drafts, three different editing rounds, or a timeframe. Having this agreement clear from the beginning will save you a lot of miscommunication, and will ensure the process is positive for both of you.

If you don't have the budget for a logo, or if you're simply not ready to commit to one, that's totally okay! There's another option that's just as effective…

YOUR FACE

We live in a world starved for genuine connections and interactions. We're constantly pummelled with advertisements, promotions, and the white noise of faceless corporations vying for our attention. And while a beautiful logo is great to have, there are a zillion flowery logos already out there, and it's easy to see them all as a homogenous online blur. If you don't have the resources to invest in a professionally designed logo, the one thing you still have that no one else does, is your face!

And you don't have to be young or conventionally beautiful to shine for your business! Think about what YOU enjoy seeing on your Facebook or Instagram feed. Think about the growers you follow, and their smiling faces. When you see a 60-something farmer, smiling in her gardens and proudly holding an armload of blooms, do you think "hm, well she's a bit old", or do you think "gosh she looks so happy! I want that life!" Maybe you

Left: I use this photo often, for my business email account, for marketing bridal work, and for my social media accounts. The day I took these photos, I had tons of leftover market flowers with nowhere to go, so I set up a mini photoshoot in my workshop space, and created as many different bridal-style bouquets as I could. The photos from that shoot have since become invaluable marketing tools.

see yourself in her (or him! Or them!).

Photograph yourself in your happy place among your blooms and all your hard work… Your audience will see themselves in you. Your face is your most effective and honest tool when it comes to reaching your markets. Take pride in your adventure! Don't be shy! You'll find a whole world of empathy and support opens up to you when you take that small vulnerable step.

Plus, it's cheaper than a logo!

KEY MESSAGES

Your Key Messages are a statement of your core beliefs and principles to your audience, followers, customers or potential partners. They're what you'll come back to again and again as your business grows and evolves. Once you've established your key messaging, your general messaging should consistently orbit those values and ideas.

Your Key Messaging should encompass:

1. Your Values

Go back to your Visioning Mind Map, and find all the words that speak to your business values. Ie: "organic", "sustainable", "family", "environment", "beauty", "care", "balance". Now write a few sentences that expand on those values, like, "We are a family focused flower farm that prioritizes balance and sustainability". Keep reworking those sentences, play with the words, see if you can narrow the concepts down into three short, concise sentences. These are now your key messages, values you will funnel into every element of your business and brand.

2. Your Story

Following the same logic as using your face as a tool to represent your business, your story is another honest and very effective way to engage with your audience, followers, and customers. It doesn't have to be your life story, and it doesn't have to be particularly detailed. It can be as simple as "I wanted a gentler life, and here I am." How much you share depends on you, and you have zero obligations to the public when it comes to sharing any personal details at all.

But, there is a curious audience ready for it, should you choose to share. Again, there is a small sea of people who want to do or support exactly what you're doing. What prompted you to begin this journey? Why did you choose this lifestyle? Summarizing your story into a paragraph or two, and making it available on your website or Facebook page offers curious customers, media, and everyone else a quick and easy place to quell their curiosity and dream along with you.

One note of caution when sharing anything personal on the internet or in the public sphere: be careful! Limit exposing minors or children who cannot consent to having their faces shared publicly. While there are thousands of wonderful people who would never dream of harming you or your family, it only takes one person to ruin your sense of security or harmony, and children are especially vulnerable.

Likewise, if you choose to share any political or religious views through your business accounts, be careful. If those views are directly related to your key messaging, then you should have a basic PR (public relations) strategy in place before sharing them. We'll get more into PR later on, but suffice to say, it's no longer possible to toss hot button opinions into the public sphere and not expect to deal with the reactions of those who disagree. Those reactions can trigger entire afternoons lost to anxiety or frustration, and drain your valuable energy. And in the world of startup businesses, time is money. Do you really want to spend X amount of dollars on someone you disagree with? And if it gets especially heated, those who choose to hassle or confront you online can put your business at risk, which is an added stress you just don't need.

Which isn't to say "never speak out about what you believe in", just plan and strategize around it, and if it isn't a part of your key messaging, it's probably more prudent to save it for conversations within your personal circles.

A cut flower farm, growing sustainably in the Alberta prairies.

Above: This is the first image that currently appears on my website's homepage. It contains all the elements of my key messaging: what we are, how we grow, and where we are.

For example, when I started Alberta Girl Acres, the word "girl" was critical. I consider myself a feminist, I'm a single mother, and I believe strongly in #womenswork, #womenwhodig and #womenwhofarm. I wrote this into my business plan, and it's part of my core messaging. While I was applying for a startup loan, an advisor asked "why Alberta GIRL Acres? What if men want to buy your product, but are put off by the word "girl"?

I almost laughed out loud, but instead I said, "anyone put off by the word "girl" is not my customer." It was that simple. And, I do have a basic PR strategy in place, in the event someone chooses to target me or my business. Coming from a background in marketing, communications, and performing,

these precautions are almost second nature to me, and their value has been evident over and over again throughout my professional online work.

3. Your Product and Target Market

Once you've established WHO you are, and WHY you're doing what you're doing, it's important to be very clear about WHAT you're selling, and WHO you're selling to. Ie: "Locally grown blooms perfect for your wedding or special event", or "Wholesale blooms serving Alberta florists", or "Market Bouquets every Saturday at the Farmer's Market". We'll get into target markets later, and once you have a clearer picture of who you want to serve and how, you can come back to writing this piece of your messaging.

48

The Alberta Girl Acres' logo, designed by Kiarra Albina. It contains all of my favourite elements of our farm, such as the old farmhouse, wild roses lining the driveway, and pink cotton candy-esque clouds.

How can we help you?

Name *

Email *

Subject

Message

Send

info@albertagirlacres.com

Communications

The term "Communications" may seem a bit overwhelming to someone outside the field. For the purposes of your startup business, it isn't too complicated, and most of the tips I'll share fall within the realm of common sense.

Email:

We all know how to use email. It's the steadfast mode of correspondence for many, and having an email address assigned to your business is an important piece of presenting yourself professionally.

In your first year, if having an email address connected to your website domain feels too complicated (ie: me@flowerbusiness.com), most people won't blink at a gmail address,

as long as it includes your business name in the address (ie: flowerbusiness@gmail.com). As your business becomes more established, you'll eventually want to switch to a more professional looking email account tied to your website.

For myself, I keep my business and personal email completely separate, so when I see X number of unread emails, I know whether they're work-related or personal.

Website "Contact" Form:

We'll get more into websites later, but the key purpose of having a website, if for no other reason, is to give people a streamlined way to contact you. In my first year, about 95%

of my inquiries and sales came from contact forms provided on my website. On many web building platforms, it's very easy to plug your email address into the form, so that inquiries are forwarded directly to your inbox. It's also a great alternative to providing your phone number publicly, which can result in incessant and annoying spam calls.

Phone Number:

In this technological climate, when people seem to be able to connect online in every way possible, treat your phone number as a precious commodity. Phone calls demand your immediate attention, can interrupt you at any time, and checking voicemails is yet another task on your long list of administrative duties as a business owner. For me, emails are far more convenient. Providing your phone number publicly, on your website and social media, will also attract heaps of spam calls. There is no "I'm not a robot" captcha filter before seeker bots find and list your phone number with various spammy call centres.

I find the best place for a phone number is on your business card, because it's offline and you know exactly who is receiving it. Florists, potential customers and partners, other growers… these are the people you want to be able to call you. Otherwise, general inquiries are always best directed into your email, which people should be able to find by searching your website or social media.

Social Media:

This one is a beast. Despite its pluses and minuses, everyone is on social media, and using it has become a critical piece of doing business. In this section, we'll talk about social media in terms of communications. Later, we'll discuss using social media as a marketing tool (p.131).

Many customers use social media in lieu of email, which can become cumbersome when you're busy with other tasks, and keeping track of messages between several platforms is a huge pain, especially because a lot of people's social media handles aren't their actual names. However, ignoring comments and direct messages will lower your online engagement, and you need that engagement, because it means more people will have a front row seat when it comes time for you to announce important news. What to do? Ack!

Auto replies are marginally better than ignoring, but the reason people engage on social media is to engage with you.

But, given the addictive nature of smartphones and social media, it's very easy to lose hours responding to comments and messages (and then scrolling through all the other farms that seem prettier and more successful than yours, gah!). Before you know it, you've lost an entire afternoon, and the giant pile of harvest buckets that needed washing have now bumped the evening harvest a few hours later than planned, and bedtime is edging closer to midnight. Double ack!

While responding IS important, it's also important to set rules for yourself. During the busy season, set Facebook auto-replies during field hours that let people know you're in the field and will respond at your earliest convenience. For Instagram and other platforms, simply decide which hours you are able to engage, and try to stick to that schedule.

When people inquire about orders or other business-related issues via social media, I almost always redirect them to my website or my email address, so I have their full names, plus the details of their inquiry in my inbox where I can more easily access it later on. There's nothing worse than sifting through Instagram messages trying to figure out who contacted you and what they needed. Business inquiries belong in your inbox, so train people to send them there.

And perhaps most importantly, keep your business accounts and personal accounts separate. Your personal accounts should serve as small reprieves, where you can connect with friends and switch off work for a while. Of course you can share bits of your life through your business account, and vice versa, and it will often FEEL like there's no divide between the two worlds, but keeping them separate will serve you well during the times when you need a break. Consider it an act of self care and self preservation. Your future self will thank you.

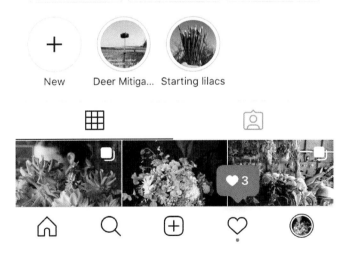

albertagirlacres ∨

300 profile visits in the last 7 days

880 Posts   **4,412** Followers   **475** Following

Alberta Girl Acres
Farm
Sarah Adams ❀ Flower Farmer

Seasonal Cut Blooms & Workshops... more
www.albertagirlacres.com
Vulcan, Alberta

| Edit Profile | Promotions | Email |

New   Deer Mitiga...   Starting lilacs

Social media can demand a lot of your attention. Put policies in place to keep your communications clear.

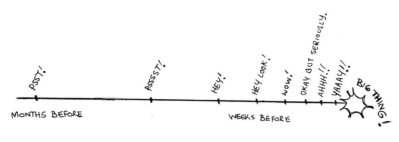

HYPE TIMELINE

THE ART OF A GOOD LAUNCH

So you have a new product or service, and you want to tell the world! Maybe you've decided to add soap or honey to your product line, or maybe you're ready to share news of your CSAs or workshops. Maybe you just want to announce your farm is open for business! Whatever news you need to share, people need to know!

"Launching" isn't just for books and rocket ships. If you have a new, important bit of business that needs to be heard, planning the news as a "launch" is a very clean and effective way to market it to your public. And while launching is very closely tied to marketing, it's far more about effective communication strategies. Timing, preparing modes of contact, and ensuring every transaction is a smooth one from start to finish, is what makes an effective launch. There are also "soft" launches and "hard" launches, and each serve very specific

purposes within your communication strategy.

The Soft Launch

A soft launch is when you spread the word of new products or services among your limited circles, whether family, co-workers, or your social media circles. No advertising is launched along with the news, no media is reached out to, and messaging of the new products or services remain minimal on your website and social media accounts.

The purpose of a soft launch is to pique the interest of those closest to you; it's a chance to share news using your own voice. Soft launches are cool, casual ways to say "oh by the way... this amazing thing is happening soon...stay tuned because it's going to be the best".

It shouldn't be *too* casual though. The purpose

of a soft launch is also to signal "THIS IS HAPPENING", whether to your public, or even just to yourself. A soft launch should also include a date promising full details, which signals commitment, and can often function as a self-inflicted boot in the butt, making all your plans and deadlines "REAL".

Inquiries may begin trickling in. Maybe you'll find a waiting list is in order to keep track of everyone who indicates interest. A soft launch is also a great way to gather newsletter subscribers; if you have an easy sign-up system, everyone curious for more news will eagerly subscribe. This sets you up very well for the next phase: the "hard" launch.

The Hard Launch

So you've piqued, teased, and hinted, and you now have several curious eyes turned in your direction. Your messaging is ready, the website is ready, the contact forms are ready, and most importantly, your products or services are ready. Every gear is greased, every ball is poised and ready to roll. The promised date arrives... it's time to sound the trumpets and launch this baby.

PRODUCTS! SERVICES! SPARKLES! MAGIC! Give em the ol' razzle dazzle, in whatever form that takes for you and your business.

A hard launch should be so well-prepared, that it's simply a process of flicking on a few switches. Prep is done: website updates; registration forms; online shops; all relevant

channels open and ready. Then off goes the newsletter (if you have a newsletter, always send it first! Your subscribers deserve the first look!), up go the social media posts, and the "boosted" content or social media advertising are put to work.

Want to take the launch one step further? Throw a party. It doesn't have to be a big deal, and it should be relevant to the product or service you're launching. Ie:

- Open your farm to the public for a Saturday afternoon BBQ to meet local flower lovers and curious neighbours.
- Invite last year's CSA members for a farm-to-table dinner.
- Have a "florists only" wine, cheese, and flowers night where you can show off your beauties and woo potential friends.
- Do a mini bridal fair!

Just remember a party comes with certain expenses, so plan and weigh it carefully! What is its purpose? What are its goals? Maybe collaborate with other growers to share the load and rewards! And be sure to encourage your guests to take photos and share the event on their personal accounts! Strategically place little signs with your @handle around the event, to remind folks to share!

But spreading big news doesn't begin and end with a launch. This is where your Communications Strategy comes into play, to ensure your audience stays keen and engaged not just during the big announcement, but over the coming weeks and months as well.

Timing

Timing when you share your news is almost as important as what you're sharing. There are certain times you're much more likely to reach a broader audience, and certain times you're much less likely. We're going to talk about daily timing, weekly timing, and yearly timing.

Daily Timing

If you're a numbers person, you might be keen to peek at your social media "insights" or "analytics" from time to time. These numbers are only offered via business accounts, another great reason to establish your own.

One thing you may notice immediately is that people are more engaged with your content at certain times of the day. If you aren't familiar with deciphering engagement analytics, I'll offer a quick summary:

It's a rather bleak fact that many of us are addicted to our smartphones, **BUT** when you join the world of small business, that addiction can actually begin to work in your favour (I know it seems horrible to exploit an addiction in the name of small business! But we all gotta eat?). A lot of people sleep with their smartphones next to their beds, using them as alarms, checking them first thing in the morning, throughout the day, and in the evenings while unwinding. So the first question you need to ask yourself, is where do you want to fit into their day?

Consider what you're sharing: pretty blooms; lighthearted loveliness; soft glimpses of a sun streaked dream? You'll want that content greeting folks first thing, as they're rising and preparing for the day ahead. These posts will do best between 6am and 8am

Calls to action? Exciting new sales? You want folks to be AWAKE before you hammer them with your big fun news, but you don't want the day to have swallowed them too completely. 8am to 10am is the best time to share important news.

Soft launches? Quiet mullings and ruminations? Questions to others in the community? This kind of content will land best between 10am and 1pm, or 7pm to 9pm. Lunch breaks, quiet evenings, etc.

The WORST times to share, in terms of engagement, is 4pm to 6pm (rush hour, aka: "oh my god can this day just be over already"), and in the middle of the night (obviously).

Weekly Timing

Low pressure, light and lovely posts are great for every day of the week, but if you're planning a hard launch, Monday is hands down the best day to release your news into the world. Most people follow weekly, cyclical routines, "resetting" each weekend. It's also no secret that Mondays are a bummer in office culture, so be their shining light. Mondays are also the days when stay-at-home parents might be taking some much anticipated quiet time from their school-aged children, so likewise, be their lovely little reprieve. For work-at-home folks, Monday is the day many are getting "back into it", and are mentally organizing the week ahead. Get in there! If you can't hit a Monday, the earlier in the week the better.

Unless it's a holiday Monday, which would make Tuesday the next best alternative. If that Monday is a BIG holiday however (ie Easter, Mother's Day, Christmas), be sure to launch any relevant news at least a week before, along with a reminder the Friday morning leading up to the special Monday.

The WORST time to launch is Friday or Saturday evening. However, I've been guilty of sending news into the world around those times, simply because it was the only time I had to share it! Remember, these are all just guidelines. Don't beat yourself up if you can't hold to your super tight comm strategy!

Yearly Timing

Every major holiday you plan to sell around should have its own little communications strategy. Sometimes you'll want to begin hyping a week or two ahead of the holiday (Valentine's Day), and sometimes you'll want to be sparkling a month or more in advance (Christmas).

You'll obviously set your own dates and hone your own messaging, but easing and teasing people into your awesome news is the most effective way to build buzz and get others pumped for your adventures! And of course, be sure to thank people afterwards!

And listen, sometimes we lose track, miss key windows, or are simply too busy to adhere to a perfect communications strategy. That's okay! Just do your best! It's better to get the news out there than not at all. The best favour you can do for yourself is setting up all your communications processes (website, email, contact forms) during the quiet bits of the year, so that when things get busy, you can at least point people straight to your inbox, rather than managing a jumble of inquiries during peak times.

You can also use platforms such as Hootsuite to manage and schedule all your posts, which is extremely useful for those good at planning! However, during your early years, you may find that plans change very quickly, and sometimes very significantly! The last thing you want is a forgotten, scheduled post blasting onto your accounts and confusing your followers.

Keep your plans loose and adaptable, with a basic communications plan in the back of your mind as you navigate these chaotic early years of growing for profit. Create a strategy for the really important bits, and then get a feel for the rest as you go.

New Message — ↗ ✕

Recipients

Subject

Sarah Adams
Owner, Alberta Girl Acres
@albertagirlacres
www.albertagirlacres.com

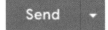   

BUSINESS COMMUNICATIONS ETIQUETTE

Throughout all your business dealings, maintaining professional etiquette is very important. The basic rules I've gleaned from my career in communications are:

1. Email salutations and signatures:

Begin emails with "Hi (Name)," and end with something simple like "Best," or "Thanks," and then your automatic business signature, which should include your name, your title, your business name, your website, and your logo. Once again, including your phone number is up to you. Do you want to give that access to everyone you correspond with?

If you're unsure how to create automatic signatures in your email, google "how to create automatic email signatures in [email server] (ie: "gmail", "G Suite", "Outlook", etc)". There are several easy-to-follow tutorials online for almost every web-related question.

2. Timely Replies:

Most people *should* understand that you're a farmer/grower, and your days are mostly spent working very hard in your fields or gardens. That said, not all do, and some may grow impatient if they don't hear back from you within a few hours. If your workload is especially heavy, particularly during peak season, set an auto-response during field hours letting people know you received their email and will respond within 24 hours. Let them know if it's an urgent or time sensitive matter, you will respond as soon as you can.

Otherwise, when work is slower, simply reply to inquiries as promptly as you can. I like to reply within a few hours, because I dislike seeing my inbox pile up. I also take certain days "off" answering emails, ie: Sundays, because most people understand and respect that Sundays are non-business days.

If you're taking a holiday, or will be away for a period of time, set an auto-response on your email and social media letting people know when you'll be back.

3. "Reply" and "Reply All":

Only "reply all" when every person listed in the email NEEDS to see your response, ie: a group conversation. If the sender simply wants input from each individual on their list of recipients, reply to the sender only.

4. CC-ing and BCC-ing:

"CC" means "Carbon Copy", heralding back to the days when people used carbon sheets to make hard copies of correspondences (letters, invoices, receipts). If you're responding to, or sending an email that references a previous email conversation that directly impacts your current email, and it makes sense to keep the person you previously conversed with in the loop, CC that person. It's also prudent to ask the person if they'd like to be CC'd first.
From that point, each person should "reply all" to keep relevant parties in the loop.

"BCC" means "Blind Carbon Copy", and is one of your best friends when emailing workshop groups or multiple CSA members. **Unless otherwise stated, people's personal email addresses should always be kept private.** When emailing small groups of people who don't know each other and have not consented to having their personal email addresses shared, always use BCC.

5. Distribution Lists:

According to Canada's Anti-Spam Legislation, it is illegal to add any person's email address to a distribution list without their consent. This is where it's important to always provide a simple "newsletter sign up" option on your website. Having a list of willing, supportive, and curious contacts is absolutely invaluable to any business, and their information should be kept private and treated with respect.

Within distribution software like Mailchimp, Wix or G Suite, it's also possible to categorize and organize your distribution lists for multiple outreach purposes, ie: "Florists", "CSA members", "Growers", etc.

Distribution lists are a valuable tool that can save you hours of admin headaches. Use them wisely!

6. Tact and Tone:

It's helpful, and even necessary, to adopt a "business persona" for your business-related correspondences. This persona uses minimal exclamation points, is grammatically thoughtful, and knows how to graciously back out of derailed, unsavoury, or annoying correspondences.

And while you will certainly develop professional relationships where you can relax into a more casual rapport, remember that YOU are the owner, the BOSS. And while it's important to maintain a professional and approachable persona, you are also under zero obligation to put up with anyone's abuse, unprofessional behaviour, or unreasonable demands. Which brings us to…

7. Dealing with Ding Dongs:

Of course "ding dongs" is a gentler term for what we'd really like to call them. We're all familiar with the term "troll", but as the internet evolves in all its unwieldy and often terrifying glory, more and more archetypes are emerging, with the sole purpose of making your life more difficult. There are still trolls, but now we also have:

Unsolicited advice from people who have no business telling you what to do.

The best way to deal with these types is to either ignore their comments (if you can), or say "yes, those are all things I've considered, thanks!" (leave out the "thanks!" if they're repeat offenders and don't seem to take the hint). You don't owe anyone repetitive explanations or justifications for doing things the way you've chosen to do them. You're just starting out for Pete's sake!

People who think your business account is a dating site.

Yes this happens. Mostly to female business owners, but certainly to others as well. The best way to deal with those "hey pretty" messages is to ignore and block. Do not engage with them, they're weirdos (or bots, equally pointless).

Also, if someone becomes flirtatious in an unwelcome way, the best response is to simply ignore their comments. If they say something especially inappropriate, delete the comment and block them. You don't owe them a response, and engaging with them is exactly what they want.

Over-enthusiastic supporters, aka: FANS.

Having enthusiastic support is great. But polite replies don't always satisfy some people, and sometimes every minimal interaction you have with them fuels an imbalance on their end that you're either, a) THEIR BEST FRIEND, or b) Someone who will help them get ahead.

The best way to deal with these people is to start off polite, but if you see a fixation forming or if their constant prods for attention are making you uncomfortable, begin ignoring or limiting how often you respond. If they can't take the hint, or seem to take offence at your backing away, eventually you may have to be blunt with them, or block them entirely.

Unforgiving Customers

We're all doing our best, but sometimes "our best" has to contend with someone else's bad day, week, month, or year (or life!). Maintaining empathy can be difficult when you've been sweating in the fields for 10 hours, just trying to share a bit of beauty with the world.

It's also a sad fact that the adage "the customer is always right" has created a consumer culture rampant with entitlement and classist views against those working in service industries. This toxic philosophy has pushed small businesses into devaluing their products and losing valuable time and revenue while bending over backwards trying to appease demanding customers. I've especially seen this happen to small scale growers. In trying to compete with imported wholesale blooms and the standardized floral industry, we've lost sight of just how valuable our products, our skills, and our time, actually are.

So how do we avoid positioning ourselves as timid, apologetic servants in the face of an industry built on instant gratification, cheap wholesale product, and entitled consumer culture?

First off: what you're doing has REAL VALUE. You're contributing to a local economy, creating jobs, and creating a sustainable option for consumers. You're tending the earth. You're pouring hours of yourself into providing beauty and comfort via fresh, lovingly grown blooms. You're showing others how it can be done, spreading hope and joy. Those are all incredibly important contributions to this world.

As you develop your PR and HR policies, identify your professional boundaries. If an order were to go terribly wrong, how far are you willing to go to rectify it? **Create clear Terms of Service**, and ensure customers purchasing your products (ie: CSAs, wedding orders) have read and understand those terms. State that you do not tolerate abuse of any kind, and that behaviour deemed abusive or inappropriate will effectively terminate memberships, orders, or other agreements entered either by contract or in good faith.

Of course, no matter how detailed your Terms of Service are, issues will arise that you simply can't plan for. Don't shed your empathy entirely, but hold your ground. Take time to

feel for this person. Are you able to offer any compensation? Maybe a discount coupon for future purchases? If nothing seems to appease the customer, it's time to slip on your "Boss Pants" and draw the line. Let them know that if they aren't interested in any of your offers or options, they are welcome to find blooms or similar services elsewhere. Your business can't be for everyone, and your time and skills have value. Drop them, and move on.

Vile jerks, aka: Trolls.

Maybe you made a passionate post about something you care deeply about, and it resonated with people, got shared widely, and brought more attention to your business. GREAT! Except all attention is not always good attention, and many miserable people will take any opportunity to target those they perceive as "enemies" to their views. They are often simply spouting the same rhetoric as they would to anyone else they've lumped into their faceless mass of "wrong people", but that doesn't make it any less infuriating, scary, or hurtful when they target you.

The best way to deal with these people is to ignore them, screenshot whatever they've sent you (document as evidence), then block them. If they continue to harass you in other ways, continue to document each instance, and notify the police if you must.

Communications

The potential for your business is as vast as the horizons are.
Having strategies in place for its growth is key.

PUBLIC RELATIONS (PR)

While much of what we just discussed in Key Messaging (p.46) pertains directly to PR, Public Relations is much more about strategizing how you interact with the media, as well as the public at large. It's also about mitigation and drawing professional boundaries.

If you're lucky enough to be contacted by a reputable media source, it's very likely that they already have a story in mind, and you're the key piece of that story.

When word got out that my business "rescued" plants, I got a ton of media attention, each outlet building on the story that came before. It didn't matter how many times I stated "we're a CUT FLOWER FARM", the concept they all ran with was "PLANT SANCTUARY".

My inbox was flooding with requests from people hoping I'd come dig up their unwanted trees (for free), and I found I was suddenly losing control of the direction I wanted for my business. Not only that, but many of the plants I did rescue were either diseased, or didn't survive the mid-summer transplants. It was a lot of time and energy spent, for almost no return.

Granted, it got our name "out there" to some extent, but it was really just a lot of me saying "sorry, I can't do that", over and over again. A tighter PR strategy that more closely followed our key messaging would have saved me a ton of time, and a ton of money in terms of labour and gas.

Strategies around how you want to message to the public are especially important when it comes to the media. It's unlikely that a flower farm will get caught up in anything unsavoury or controversial, but in the event that anything ever becomes misconstrued (ie: an interaction with a dissatisfied customer that gets posted or shared widely without your knowledge), it's helpful to have a basic strategy in place.

A PR strategy could be as simple as "do not respond to comments without team consultation", or "block trolls immediately", or it could be a more in-depth guide provided to employees or team members, including key messages to fall back on, and clear policies re: who will respond to public inquiries, and how you want your business represented.

For example, if an employee is active on social media and is vocal about veganism, do you want them posting photos praising your flower fields and condemning cattle farms, potentially insulting the hard working farmers (and supportive agricultural allies) all around you? Maybe not. Likewise, any team member who posts anything along the lines of "we here at [your business] are all about THIS", when the point they're making doesn't really fit into your

Above: Xeranthemum, a wonderful everlasting flower. Right page: A lovely harvest of Ammi Dara, aka chocolate laceflower.

messaging.

It's great when team members take pride in your enterprise, but some don't always see the same vision as you do. It's your job to ensure YOUR vision is the one the public sees. It's your business, and the stakes are highest for you!

And as we discussed in Communications, when dealing with "unforgiving customers" it's important to create very clear Terms of Service that let your customers and clients know exactly where your business' boundaries are. Can a CSA member who paid for delivery at the beginning of the season switch to pick-up mid season, or vice versa? Can a bride request a refund a month before the wedding? You will need to create different Terms of Services for different products and services, or create one blanket policy that covers your services and capacities as well as possible. It will save you many, many headaches later on.

Left page: Our flower processing space inside one of our large outbuildings. This space also includes a DIY walk in cooler (not pictured).

Production

THINKING ECONOMICALLY

Before you've decided which markets you'd like to serve, an easily overlooked point of consideration is *what* product you will actually sell them. Every flower is not created equal when serving different market streams! In your early years, it's extremely important to consider that there are economical flowers and not so economical flowers.

For example:

DAHLIAS: The Diva of the Flower Farm

Dahlias are generally considered a high value bloom, not only because of their incredible beauty and great market value with floral designers, but because they are one of the most labour intensive flowers to grow in climates where overwintering is not an option. So their market value is high, but so is their labour value.

In my first year, I planted 400 dahlia tubers. About half of them bloomed for a month in the summer, and when the other half was just about to hit their stride, a hard frost came and ended them all (it came freakishly early, and they were protected!). I was then faced with the task of digging them all up (many tubers had doubled or tripled in bulk), dividing them, storing them, and crossing my fingers they would survive seven months of winter storage, to be replanted in the spring.

I knew this was the process, and I knew tons of other Northern growers were going through the same rigamarole. It takes a long time to dig up 400 dahlias by hand, and in your first year, it's unlikely you'll have specialized equipment to make the job easier (but if you do, more power to you!). When I factored in the weeks of labour it took to dig them up, divide, and store them, plus the fact that I only sold blooms from the plants for four weeks, they suddenly didn't look like such a high value bloom.

After working out the numbers, dahlias were looking like much more of a loss. Sure, in Year Two I would have my greenhouse to grow them in, but that would only mean more dahlias to dig, divide, and store. And during the summer, my farmers market customers honestly didn't even look twice at some of my biggest and most glorious dinner plate dahlias.

From what I was seeing on my feeds, other growers seemed to shrug and accept the massive amounts of labour that goes into growing dahlias. "Still haven't dug my dahlias!", "Ugh I'm putting off dividing my dahlias!", "We just spent three weeks sorting dahlias!". I reached out to other Northern growers to get their feedback re: whether dahlias actually made sense for our bottom lines, or whether we've all just been wooed by their beauty and celebrity nature. Some growers confessed they were their least profitable blooms, some insisted they were their best source of revenue. So what was the difference? Scale? Hired help? Experience?

Finally, an experienced Northern grower noted she gets her best prices for dahlias from designers, and it all clicked. Having floral designers as a target market, where your showstopper dahlias are not only appreciated but sought after, is obviously going to bring you a great return. The industry of custom floral work is a HIGH VALUE industry, which also demands heaps of specialized skills and services.

In my first year, my target market was not floral designers. My flowers were all direct market, and my mixed bouquets were all destined for the general public, where most folks were unlikely to value a dahlia over an aster. In choosing to sell direct market, I simply can't get a high enough price to justify those high maintenance blooms.

I do, however, get a very good price for regular and low maintenance blooms. Therefore planting, maintaining, tagging, digging, dividing, storing, and replanting dahlias does not make sense for *my* market, or *my* bottom line.

BUT I can still grow and sell beautiful dahlias! Growing dahlias from seed is a fun, inexpensive, and very easy way to fill my gardens and market bouquets with little showstoppers. I can also propagate up to twenty plants from a single "fancy" tuber in the early spring, which is a much more efficient way to grow designer varieties on a small scale. I may not be able to guarantee two dozen Cafe au Lait's for an August wedding, but I can send armloads of cheery pretties out to my flower-loving customers, and my bottom line looks just as lovely!

And there's another way to grow fancy dahlias and still get a good return, even if you don't sell to designers: host a "dig your own tubers" event in the fall, where the public is invited to come dig and purchase your lovely tubers. Your return will at least cover the initial cost of the tubers. Maybe you'll make enough to purchase your tubers for the following spring, without having to store any! Win win for everyone.

A lovely bunch of from-seed dahlias.

TULIPS: One Hit Wonders

Another deceptively alluring flower is the tulip. There are soooo many gorgeous tulips out there; peony-type doubles and parrots, in a vast variety of colours and sizes. Every time I see a grower holding an armload of gorgeous tulips I get full-on heart eyes.

I've learned through trial and error, however, that they are ultimately an indulgence flower (for the grower, not the customer). The bulbs, even at wholesale cost, are pricey, and they typically only produce ONE stem per bulb, which sells for marginally higher prices than the initial bulb cost. The fancy doubles also don't perennialize well, and in my climate, bud abortion is a serious risk each spring.

On top of all that, grocery stores and outlets like Costco are veritably flooded with imported Dutch tulips in the spring. They are everywhere, widely available and extremely cheap. There are limits to what the market will bear, and your gorgeous, buttery, double blooming beauties could easily just be passed over as "really expensive tulips". The only way I can see them being truly worth it, is if you're selling to high end designers, are a high end designer yourself, or have a reputable niche outlet to sell through. Otherwise, they simply don't pay their way.

One the other hand, ranunculus and anemones are cherished darlings of early springtime, are easy to grow, and produce multiple stems per corm, fetching an excellent price per stem (often almost double that of a standard tulip). Where you might just break even with a tulip bulb, you will make a much more satisfying return on a ranunculus corm. It's all about growing economically.

In terms of other economical flowers (ie: flowers that sell well for minimum investment/labour), perennials are a must on any cut flower farm. Specifically, perennials that bloom in the shoulder seasons, ie: spring pretties like daffodils, lilacs, delphiniums, peonies, and apple blossoms, and late fall lovelies like joe pye weed, Russian sage, stonecrop, daisies, black-eyed susans, various small berries, ornamental grasses, and eryngium. Establishing low-maintenance perennials that fill bouquets in the spring and fall gives you more breathing room when it comes to planning your more needy annuals.

And of course, there are economical annuals too! Self seeders like cosmos, amaranth, laceflower, bupleurum, Iceland poppies, sweet peas, nigella, and a host of others, make your seed starting and sowing work a touch lighter year after year. Self seeders don't give you the same control as starting and transplanting seedlings does, and I still start tons of seeds indoors every spring, but I also love seeing what pops up year after year, and I especially enjoy the natural, "gardeny" look they bring to my field and beds.

Take some time to research "biodynamic" farming as well. For some reason, many who are new to gardening have the idea that growing a garden means tilling soil into a fine, clean powder every spring, and then fertilizing and watering the crap out of everything they plant. Weeds and bugs are sprayed, and in the fall, gardens are mowed and tilled into a powdery clean slate once again. This causes the topsoil to blow away over the winter due to its airy consistency, as well as the fact that it has nothing rooting it down. Fine, powdery soil can't retain moisture, and constant tilling blasts away beneficial microbes. And then the gardener wonders why everything struggles to grow the following spring, prompting a cycle of unhealthy plants, more "miracle" fertilizer, more pesticides, etc etc.

You can be a lot lazier and have a much healthier garden! Leave plants to decompose in your beds over the winter. Use diatomaceous earth to reduce harmful insect populations. Build the soil up rather than constantly tilling it. Introduce beneficial insects, use cover crops and temporary landscape fabric, and most importantly, know your plants!

But this isn't a book about growing (perhaps I'll write one for prairie growers soon, I'll call it "Lazy Gardening for One"!), it's about setting up your business. Be sure to measure *what* you're growing against *who* you're selling to, and *how* you're selling it. The value of your output MUST be compatible with the value of your input. And labour counts! Time is money!

In terms of small scale growing practices, it's my opinion that the best course you can currently take re: cut flower production is the Floret Online Workshop. If you're an amateur grower and are looking for answers when it comes to plant spacing, bed yields, succession planting, harvest practices, and post-harvest care, the Floret course is everything you'll ever need. I also highly recommend Jean-Martin Fortier's The Market Gardener as an excellent guide on organic small scale growing for profit.

SCALE & CAPACITY

Every farm or growing plot is different, but I'll share the basic details of our first year in production:

Growing on 1/4 acre, we moved 50 bouquets per week during the spring, and about 70 bouquets per week during the summer months. Because it was mostly just me and my one hired farm hand, it was also the maximum amount we could handle labour-wise, as we awkwardly learned each method and process from scratch, building farm infrastructure as we went. At 70 bouquets per week, we were stretched to maximum capacity.

However, almost half of those bouquets were allocated to CSAs, which had already been paid for in the spring. So, on average, we were selling 20 - 40 bouquets at the market per week, at $20 each. On average, we made about $600 per week from our Saturday market bouquets.

Above: For us, ranunculus are a much more economical flower than tulips. They are beautiful, high value, and grow multiple stems per plant. Their corms multiply each season, and are easy to dig and save in colder zones.

Most of our spring bulbs didn't come up in May (they had been hurriedly planted the previous fall, a week before the ground froze solid), and the frost ended our production in early September, so we were really only in full production from June to the end of August. In May and June, I foraged, which was a massive amount of work, and something I'll touch on later in this section.

While the CSAs sometimes felt like they were draining our market sales, they were also *critical* to spreading the word in our first year. For every CSA member, we easily gained another new customer, sometimes several.

Deciding on your scale from the get-go is the first step in determining how much you can feasibly produce, and in turn, sell. If your family already owns a farm, and it's equipped with everything you need to get growing, an acre might not seem overwhelming. However keep in mind you'll need space to start seeds (unless you choose to direct seed everything, which is fine too, it just means a shorter bloom window for most flowers), and you'll need help to weed, harvest and process all those blooms.

If you're thinking of turning a backyard space into a profitable cut garden, you may want to focus on higher value blooms, and your first year might rely more on creating relationships with florists and designers.

That said, some backyard plots may certainly be large enough to sustain enough flowers for broader market sales, and if your house is zoned for home-based businesses, you could potentially run plenty of workshops too! Smaller scale also comes with fewer startup equipment and infrastructure costs, but might not necessarily means fewer labour costs.

The scale of your business really depends on your available resources, your ambitions and your vision. The most reliable advice is to "start small", however that doesn't mean you can't dream big! Your business plan is a road map to all your dreamiest ambitions, it may not all happen in the first year, and your plans may change significantly from year to year, but the business you're building will eventually mirror your commitment and passion.

AMBITION VS. REALITY

When considering your capacity, it's easy to overestimate how much you can handle on your own. One of my biggest personal foibles is my ability to create rose-tinted plans, where everything looks just dandy on paper, but relies almost entirely on everything working out exactly as planned. Farms don't work that way. Businesses don't either. A farming business? It will do its best to confound you at every turn. That's why it's extremely important to be patient, start slow, and weigh out your capacity as you go.

PROFIT PER PLANT

Starting out, it's really hard to predict exactly how much money each plot or plant will generate. There are so many factors that come into play, ie: weather, pests, soil health, labour, post-harvest care, local market value… there are online resources that share general market values in different areas for organic produce and flowers (ask your local wholesalers or agricultural agencies), but if you're hoping to accurately project per stem profits, you might just drive yourself a bit mad.

As you gain growing experience, you'll start to get a better feel for what grows well for you and your climate, and you'll be able to predict your crop's profits much more reliably. It takes quite a bit of trial and error though, so don't bank too hard on your first year crops by comparing expected blooms to wholesale price lists (we'll discuss this more in Pricing, p.78).

Since I began researching market farming years ago, the concept that really stuck with me was "cost vs. revenue per square foot". In terms of ballpark estimating, I find this is a more reliable point to start from. It's also one of the reasons flowers ultimately triumphed over veggies while I was deciding what I wanted to grow.

For example, pumpkins and ornamental squash seem like nice things to grow right? People love them in the fall, and nothing is funner than a pumpkin patch.

BUT, how much garden space does a pumpkin plant take up? A LOT. And how hungry and thirsty are pumpkin plants? VERY. And how

76

Chater's double hollyhocks were a wonderful surprise success for us. Their pom pom blooms are exquisite.

much can you sell a pumpkin or ornamental squash for? $2.00? $5.00? Maybe $10.00 for a big one? That's not a great return considering how much garden space they're using.

Likewise with carrots, chard, etc. A 2lb bag of farmer's market carrots sells for about $4.50. And how many square feet do they require to grow? How long do they take to mature?

Cut flowers are a wonderful small scale crop because many of them are cut-and-come-again, meaning you can snip several blooms from one plant over the season. A cosmos plant or branching sunflower could potentially yield $10 - $30 per plant, and a plant doesn't take up more than one or two square feet, especially if you're growing using intensive-spacing methods (recommended!).

In my first year, I simply grew everything I could, while loosely keeping in mind succession planting and establishing perennials. I had taken the Floret Online Workshop, and knew all the things I should be doing, but did I have the time or budget to do every single thing exactly how it should be done? Nope!

Researching, locating supplies, connecting with helpful resources, building infrastructure… those things all take time, and when my planning window closed and the warm weather meant it was time to start working outdoors 12 hours a day, the best I could do was say "WELP, HERE WE GO" and power forward into the great unknown.

The most common advice I've heard from experienced growers is to overplant. Grow way more than you think you'll need. You'll learn more about what grows well and what doesn't, and if a certain crop goes awry, you'll have plenty more to fall back on.

You may also find success in unexpected places. Depending on what's in demand in your region, you may accidentally discover a very reliable market for pussy willows, crabapple branches, or even grain crops used for ornamental purposes. Grasses are huge for florists, as are greenery and foliage. Keep an open mind during your first year, and see what opportunities pop up!

Pricing Your Flowers

One of the biggest blunders I see newbie growers make is drastically undervaluing their flowers. When I started, I honestly had no idea what to charge for my blooms, and I was very insecure when customers would ask "how much?". It wasn't until my second year, when I connected with a generous and very supportive florist, that I started to see just how much I was undervaluing my flowers (and my hard work!). She provided me with wholesale lists from BC suppliers, and after reviewing those lists, I literally put my head in my hands and groaned at how grossly I had undersold my flowers the year before.

Having wholesale lists to reference was a place to start, but they still couldn't dictate how I priced *my* flowers. There were many factors to consider, the main one being that, in Alberta, our growing season is basically four months of the year. We also have harsher weather in the prairies, such as high winds, drought, and powerful storms. A lot of people out here assume we just can't grow anything due to such extreme conditions. So, for a Northern prairie grower to produce a lovely crop of dahlias? It takes a ton of work, more infrastructure (low/high tunnels, wind and hail mitigation), and we only have them for a very brief time. The scarcity of our locally grown blooms means their value is intrinsically higher. To set prices for our flowers, we must account for our climate and our labour. This holds true for small scale growers in any other locations.

Imported, wholesale flowers from commercial scale operations are a *different product* than local market farm flowers. Their value cannot be compared. Small scale farms do not have industrial processes in place. Our budgets are tiny, our revenue feeds our families directly, and our practices are specialized. Every flower is not created equal, no matter what the standardized floral industry may tell you.

I've also seen "success" stories pop up in my online flower farming groups, where a new grower has approached a florist for the first time, and the florist "bought everything on the spot!". First off, that's great! Buuut... if you're undervaluing your flowers, offering high quality product for 50% less (or lower) than what a florist is currently paying for their wholesale flowers, OF COURSE they're going

Above: Anemones peeking up in the greenhouse. They are one of our earliest producers.

to jump at your blooms. And of course they'll want plenty more! They're getting top quality product for dirt cheap! And are those sales enough to cover your costs? Your labour? Are you making enough on those sales that at the end of the year, your budget is balanced and you've made a profit? Probably not.

Listen, you're the boss of your flowers. You're growing carefully tended, unique, loved blooms. Would an artisanal bakery base their bread prices on Safeway's? No. You get to set the value of your blooms, because you're not selling just any old flowers, you're selling a superior product.

That said, if you're planning to sell at a small

Above: Peachy and salmon from-seed dahlias.

rural farmer's market, you can't demand $6/ bloom. If you're setting up a flower stand at the end of your driveway, you likely won't get $75 for a bouquet. This is why it's important to think hard about your market, before you've grown a single flower. Considering the economical virtues of your flowers first will go a long way.

So where do we start when pricing our flowers? Referencing wholesale lists is important, but it's certainly not the end of the equation for small scale growers.

My basic pricing system works like this:

WHOLESALE:

If you have a business number, start an account with a floral wholesale supplier, and ask to receive updated lists. Based on those lists, let's say the wholesale price for an imported

campanula stem is .60 cents.

Factoring in my climate and my labour, I add 50%. Now, my wholesale price for a campanula stem is .90 cents. This is my price for florists.

If I'm selling bunches to a grocery store, I would charge according to my wholesale price for each stem, so I would be asking the grocery store for about $9.00 per 10 stem bunch (depending on the flower).

If I'm selling mixed bouquets to a grocery store, I would mark up my wholesale cost by 30% to account for additional labour. The grocery store would pay me about $11.70 for a small, 10 stem bouquet. A larger, 20 stem bouquet would cost the grocery store around $23.50, and so on. The grocery outlets would then mark up further to make their profit.

However, if a grocery store was willing to offer a seasonal contract, with 50% paid upfront and 50% mid season, I would offer my flowers to them at slightly lower wholesale prices. The reliability of the revenue would be worth the trade, in my opinion. That said, DO NOT sign a contract in your first year. Wait until you have reliable production and consistent processes.

These prices are not set in stone, obviously, but they are my minimum prices if I want to receive any return on my blooms.

DIRECT MARKET:

Now, if I choose to sell bunches at a farmer's market or a farm stand, I will mark up anywhere from 30% to 100%, depending on what my market can bear; consider rural vs urban, walking traffic, population density and demographics, which we'll discuss more in "Identifying Your Market" (p.105). Now our campanula stem is somewhere between $1.17 and $1.80 per stem. A bunch of 10 stems would cost anywhere from $11.70 to $18.00.

If I'm creating market bouquets, I'm going to factor in my additional labour costs, marking up anywhere from 50% to 100%, again depending on what my market can bear. If it's a straightforward, made-for-market, 20 stem bouquet (made from stems of similar value), I will price it around $35.00.

CUSTOM DESIGN:

For general custom requests (ie: "Can you make something nice for my mom? She loves dahlias and sunflowers."), I mark up by about 150% from my wholesale prices, assuming the customer service will be minimal. So a custom gift bouquet would cost from $45 to $100, depending on flowers used and stem count.

ANY special event request (ie: a wedding bouquet or a special anniversary arrangement) should be marked up by about 300% from your wholesale price, to factor in the additional labour, skill, and customer service this order will entail. A bride's bouquet typically falls around the $125 to $300 range, depending on stem count and flowers used.

If floral design is your thing, you can adjust or raise your prices according to your design experience and demand. For myself, I don't mind charging higher prices for custom work, because while I'm good at the design part, customer service isn't something I particularly enjoy. If I'm going to do it at all, I want to be paid well for my time.

SEASONAL PRICING:

This is another very important factor to consider when pricing your product. Springtime in Canada means plenty of tulips, daffodils, ranunculus, anemones, lilacs, etc. All these flowers are considered "in season" in the spring. A Canadian-grown dahlia blooming in April would be quite a feat, involving a heated greenhouse at least. The costs to produce that dahlia would be much higher, so the value of that flower goes way up.

Producing out-of-season, local flowers in a heated greenhouse might seem like a goldmine idea at first, but remember, you can still only sell at prices your local market will bear. If a florist is getting roses from Equador in April for $1.25/stem, and you pop in with "local roses!" that actually cost you $7/stem to grow (factoring in heating costs for the greenhouse, as well as labour. etc), the florist will most likely say "Wow neat! I can't afford that though, sorry!" If the *most* you can sell that "out of season, locally grown" rose for is $2.50/stem, you'll end up taking a significant loss on that lovely greenhouse crop.

That said, unheated season extenders are a great way to get a good return on your shoulder-season flowers, as you'll have blooms

81

a good two to six weeks before the field-grown flowers get started. And as we noted before, perennials and cut-and-come-again flowers are always the best return for your labour.

In terms of how much revenue my farm was able to generate in our first year, here's a basic breakdown:

Product/Service	Gross Revenue
Market Bouquets	$6500
CSAs	$7000
Workshops & Classes	$9500
On Farm Sales	$250
Winter Projects	$1000

In total, growing on a quarter acre, my farm grossed just under $25 000 in our first year.

In our second year, we doubled that number, grossing about $55 000. We were also growing on a full acre, however the added bed space didn't necessarily add up to higher revenue. A more established customer base, getting a better feel for our strengths, and established, more efficient processes all contributed to a healthier gross revenue.

As we continue into our farm's evolution, my aim is to keep labour requirements low, while focusing on efficient processes and products

and services that I legitimately enjoy. I don't want my farm to grow beyond what feels right for *me*. I'm a private person, who really just loves gardening, creating, and teaching. I don't want to become a large scale wholesale supplier, a sought after floral designer, a wedding planner, or an employer of dozens. I want to have a beautiful farm that I can share with people who appreciate it. If I can do that while paying my bills, that sounds just about perfect to me.

Below: A quick example of the wholesale list I provide to grocery stores. While supplying grocery stores isn't a focal point of my business plan, I keep updated lists for the occasional times that a store will inquire.

SEASONAL BOUQUETS			Wholesale Cost
SMALL - 10 STEMS			$9.50
MEDIUM - 20 STEMS			$15.00
LARGE - 35 STEMS			$20.00

This list is an example of what may be available throughout the season. All varieties may not be available on a consistent weekly basis.

Stems/Bunch

BUNCHES - VARIETY	BUNCHES COUNT		Wholesale Cost
ALLIUM, GLOBE	BU (5)		$6.90
ANEMONE, ASST	BU (10)		$13.23
ANEMONE, WHITE, BLUSH	BU (10)		$16.10
AMARANTHUS, SPIKE	BU (5)		$5.75
AMARANTHUS, HANGING	BU (5)		$6.33
ASTER, KING SIZED	BU (5)		$6.04
ASTER, MED	BU (5)		$5.46
ASTER, MINI	BU (10)		$8.05
BELLS OF IRELAND	BU (10)		$11.50
BORAGE, FLOWERING	BU (10)		$8.05
CALENDULA, LONG STEM	BU (10)		$9.20
CLEMATIS	BU (5)		$5.18
COLUMBINE	BU (10)		$6.90
CORN FLOWER	BU (10)		$6.90

Left page: Wolf willow grows wild throughout the Northern prairies, and works beautifully as bouquet foliage.

FORAGING

In the early months of our first year, I ended up foraging to create enough bouquets to make a spring showing at the farmers' market, and to fulfill our promised CSA shares. Foraging was never "in the plan" however, and I resorted to it only out of pure panic as winter lasted almost five weeks longer than usual, setting our production back and putting us way behind in terms of starting a revenue stream.

The stress of those first few weeks, driving for hours on end scouting out wildflower patches I could legally cut from… I wouldn't wish that pressure on anyone. Had I known spring was going to be SO late (how could I though?) I would have made an early plea to all my friends with large yards and perennial gardens, and simply cut from them as long as I was able. In the midst of the chaos, I did indeed reach out to a few gardener friends, and they helped me immensely, but I could have planned much better for that particular emergency, and I would certainly urge other first year growers to mitigate such circumstances through careful planning.

If you happen to have established perennials, woodies, and foliage already growing on your property, you'll find they will quickly become part of your spring sales. Not sure what will last in the vase? Don't waste too much time asking questions online, simply go take cuttings and see how they do!

There are foraging Rules and foraging Ethics, and both must be considered before foraging wild plants, both within and beyond your property's borders.

THE RULES

Each country, province, or state will have its own laws, but in Canada, it is illegal to cut flowers or take plants from national or provincial parks, indigenous reserves, and others' private property (obviously). If you decide to go on a wildflower foraging adventure, always research where those boundaries are first.

It should go without saying, but trespassing is a BIG no-no. Even if you see yarrow growing just beyond the thin wire fence of a thousand-acre field, unless the owner of that land has given you express permission to enter and forage, slipping past the fence is trespassing. Don't do it.

85

Additionally, each province or state has lists of endangered plants that may not be disturbed, as well as noxious invasive plants that may not be harvested, propagated, or sold in any way.

I can't tell you how thrilled I was to find ditches full of thriving wild baby's breath (it smells like chocolate!), and then how heartbroken I was to discover it was a noxious invasive in Alberta. It was SO HARD to let my beautiful clouds of sweet bouquet filler go.

You should also research each and every plant before you pluck it, as there are several very beautiful, but VERY toxic wildflowers. Be sure to know what's what before cutting, or use a bit of cellphone data and check as you go!

THE ETHICS

Bees need wildflowers, and so do a zillion other creatures. And we need pollinators! A general rule of thumb is to cut only one of every ten wildflowers, leaving plenty for our friends. The only time I disregarded this rule was when the county began its annual practice of mowing roadside ditches, many of which were filled with yarrow and wild sunflowers. In those instances, I gathered what I could, often a day or two before they were mowed.

Also never harvest or disturb the roots! Leave them be, let them continue to develop and thrive in their natural ecosystems.

In my opinion, selling foraged plants and wildflowers for profit is fairly ethically iffy, and honestly if I hadn't been in sheer panic mode during those early weeks, I would have avoided it altogether. I've since turned my efforts to establishing as many perennials and fast-growing foliage as I can on our farm, which, paired with our greenhouse and low tunnels, should mitigate having to scour the prairie countryside looking for wild pretties ever again.

The most helpful and fruitful resource for foraging was simply generous gardener friends, or buddies who had inherited neglected perennial-filled yards and didn't mind visits from their frazzled farmer friend. That, and alfalfa from our farm's fields, worked wonderfully as bouquet filler.

Honestly, foraging is a TON of work. If anything, the blooms I gathered while foraging were at least twice as labour intensive than our farm grown flowers (which includes starting seeds and digging beds!), and incredibly more stressful. Not to mention expensive, due to fuel consumption and all the time I was pulled away from the farm.

There are no "free flowers". If you choose to forage, know the rules and ethics first, and approach it with a respectful mindset. Ultimately, you're far better off propagating wildflower favourites in your own gardens.

Right page: Foraged prairie smoke geum.

Left page: A beautiful arrangement created during one of our summer workshops.

Your Products & Services

When you imagine running a flower farm, it's easy to assume your primary product will be fresh flowers, right? I mean, it's a FLOWER farm, and growing flowers for profit is the goal. But "flowers" can encompass a whole world of products and services, and diversifying your revenue streams is extremely important when it comes to surviving on a small scale.

So let's start with the obvious:

Fresh Flowers

Bunches, bouquets, and single stems are really what your operation is most likely to revolve around. They're also the most glamorous product that will fill your social media feeds, promotional materials, and other online marketing. They are the stars of the show, no doubt.

But when all the numbers are added up at the end of your season, they might not always fetch the best return. In your early years – growing on a small scale, still establishing your infrastructure and your customer base – producing reliable, long-stemmed beauties, and then selling them all, is a big challenge.

And depending how long your growing season is, you may find you only have fresh blooms available for two or three months of the year. Season extenders like greenhouses and low tunnels help, but even if your flowers are generating $1000 per week (which is very optimistic for a first year grower), if you're only growing them for five months of the year, that equals about $20 000 in revenue.

Note that I say "revenue" and not "profit". Profit can't be counted until you've subtracted all your expenses from that revenue. So subtracting the expense of your greenhouse, low tunnels, seeds, bulbs, compost, netting, tools, equipment, labour, etc... how much profit is left? Not to mention your personal

Above: Paper daisies are a wonderful everlasting flower. The flowers pictured here were fully dried.

expenses, such as your rent or mortgage, food, bills, etc. Not many people can live on $20 000 a year, and even fewer can run a farm on it.

So while your fresh flowers play an extremely important role in marketing and representing your business, they shouldn't be counted on to carry you exclusively. They are massively labour intensive, and finding a way to stretch their value further is extremely important. Growing on a small scale, in a limited season, making every bloom count is the only way to ensure your business remains financially sustainable.

Dried and Pressed Flowers

If you're a short season grower, the biggest favour you can do for yourself is dry, dry, dry. Not sure if it'll dry well? Dry it anyway. I've often had people ask me which flowers dry best, and my response is always "what do you want them for?". I dry everything, because

every flower offers something different. Texture, colour, shape... I'm not going to sell perfectly preserved flowers in December, and my customers know that. Create a basic hanging rack for unsold market blooms, and dry everything you can. It's extremely easy to do, and you'll be amazed at how much beauty you've gifted yourself with when the growing season ends.

The revenue possibilities for dried flowers are vast. Bouquets, bunches, wreaths, floral crowns, hair pins, art works, stationary, grandma's favourite potpourri...if you have even a speck of creativity in you, you can find a way to use dried flowers. They usually don't require expensive equipment or supplies, they store almost indefinitely, and they're a wonderful way to generate revenue in the off season. You can hang them in the dark to preserve colour, bury them gently in silica sand to preserve their shape, press them for paper crafts, sun bleach them for wintery wreaths, or create mixes of brightly coloured petals for wedding confetti. There are just so many options!

They're also an extremely satisfying way to process unsold blooms. I used to come home from slow days at the farmer's market with buckets of unsold flowers feeling utterly defeated, but once I caught on to dried flowers, I didn't care anymore! They went straight to the drying racks, and I imagined what I could use them for in the winter. Those unsold blooms still had value. Plus, rather than composting deadheaded flowers, I could dry them! Short stems? Dry em! Gone to seed? Dry em! Set up a basic string or wire rack in a dark space (basements work great), and dry, dry, dry.

And this doesn't only apply to short season growers! If you're growing in zone 10, why not dry flowers too? They're less demanding in terms of infrastructure (no coolers, hydrators, or holding solutions needed), less work in terms of marketing (no hustling them to the florist or market while they're still fresh) and there's a legitimate demand for them.

Edible Flowers

There are pros and cons to growing edible flowers. From the outset, they seem like a fun way to market blooms in a creative way. "Eat your bouquet!", "A flowery salad!". I still dream of the day when I can specialize in offering an entirely edible line of CSA bouquet subscriptions.

But hold up. The second you advertise that your business is selling something edible, a whole avalanche of health and safety concerns come rolling in. The liabilities and legalities that appear with any edible product will throw your business plan into an entirely new realm of permits and licensing. This book isn't a guide to setting up a restaurant or eatery, and we're not going to go into great depth when it comes to setting up a business for edible product. Suffice to say, you can't just decide to start advertising and selling "edible" anything. You must go through the proper channels and ensure you are meeting all the requirements of your government's, or your farmer's market's, health and safety regulations. These regulations may differ from market to market, province to province, and state to state, but be sure to do your research and speak to other small scale food producers in your area before going ahead with edibles.

Seeds

In my first year, seeds seemed like a great possible revenue stream, but I honestly had no idea what was going to grow reliably enough to produce enough seeds to sell. I also wasn't experienced enough when it came cultivating, collecting and processing seeds; many seeds won't grow true after the bloom has cross pollinated with another flower, and some seeds are patented, which means it's illegal to save or propatage them. So, not only was marketing them infeasible, but promising more than I could have delivered would have been an unnecessary risk.

91

Above: Sweet pea seeds are one of the easiest to save, and are loved by gardeners everywhere.

BUT, after a bit of research, you'll find some seeds are wonderfully low maintenance. If, at the end of your season, you happen to have a field full of sweet peas all dressed up with nowhere to go, let them go to seed! Then collect the seeds (before the pods twist and snap, flinging all your precious babies to the four corners of the earth), allow them to fully dry, and package them up for a nice little bit of side revenue before Christmas.

People LOVE seeds! They represent so much hope and promise. And by selling seeds, you also tap into a new market of gardeners, who might not have been interested in buying your flowers, but are definitely interested in buying your seeds.

The year I decided to sell seeds, I generated over $1000 from one impromptu seed sale, harvesting from a twenty foot patch of sweet peas. And that was AFTER a full season of harvesting and selling blooms from those same plants. This worked wonderfully for my short season too, since I didn't have time to succession plant new crops when the old ones faded. By selling their seeds, I was able to essentially get another flush of revenue from the same small patch.

There are basic regulations to selling seeds as well, primarily when it comes to counting them and labeling the packages. For the most part, you cannot ship seeds outside of your home country without knowing and following your country's importation/exportation regulations. But, starting out, your market is most likely to be local, which gives you plenty of time to get a feel for your seed processing and packaging methods before you branch out.

Value-added

"Value-added" can mean anything from soaps to stationary to jewellery. Any craft or piece of art you feel inspired to create can potentially add wonderful value to your pretties, and can also add a lovely revenue stream during the slow seasons.

The key things to remember when creating any value-added product are: SUPPLIES, LABOUR and RETURN. If you're using calendula to make and market natural soaps, you must account for the cost of all the supplies (calendula included!), plus the time it will take you to make them. If you're selling them for $3.00 a bar, and you've made 100 bars, $300 seems like a tidy return. But once you've factored in your supplies and labour, is there actually a profit there? Would it have been more economical to simply partner with a soap maker, supply calendula to them, and cross promote each other? Any collaboration builds your marketing network too, an added bonus!

If you do choose to sell value-added products, just make sure it's something you're proficient enough at creating, so it doesn't end up eating valuable time that could be spent elsewhere. Time is money! And if you really want to do it but it isn't a guaranteed return, count it as a personal hobby and keep it out of the business

altogether (or include it in a one-time special promotion!). Once you've mastered it, you can implement it into your business.

Or, as noted, simply collaborate with a creator who wants to support a local flower farm! Two businesses reach further than one!

Floral Design Services

Through teaching my business courses, it has become evident that many new growers envision the life of growing gorgeous blooms AND designing beautiful arrangements, living the dream of a "farmer florist". I'll admit that when I started out, I too thought this was the most obvious path.

It WOULD be lovely, wouldn't it? And really, it makes a ton of sense! You'd have total control over what you grew and how it was grown. You'd know exactly which blooms were available when, and you could (hypothetically) make a tidy profit through your arrangements. It all looks great on paper!

There's a HUGE catch, however. And that is: a flower farm and a floristry service are two very different businesses. Starting and running a flower farm is what we're covering in this book, but covering the intricacies of running a floristry business would demand a whole new book!

The industry of custom floral work demands very specialized skills not only in floral design, but more importantly, customer service.

Above: A bridal bouquet, created to showcase our wedding design services.

Floristry is a luxury service industry, which means your customers will need your attention often, and failing to meet expectations on customized requests could lead to utter devastation on the customer's end. Weddings, anniversaries, milestone events… these orders are often planned and placed several months, sometimes years in advance. There is a LOT of pressure to deliver.

If you choose to take on floral design as well as farming, find an experienced florist to mentor with first, and focus on the customer service end of the business while you learn. Designing custom flower arrangements seems very glamorous from a beginner's perspective, but disillusionment will soon set in if you haven't carefully researched and planned for the service components of running such a business. Most importantly, focus on and find your footing in ONE of the industries – growing or floristry – FIRST, then expand to the other.

Garden Design Services

One of my favourite things is when friends contact me asking for gardening advice, especially if they're new to gardening! I also love hosting cut garden planning workshops. Recommending favourites and sharing as many tips and tricks as I can, I love playing some small part in the creation of a new, beautiful garden. I should note however, that I offer free advice to friends with small gardens, but I find it very difficult to answer ongoing flower farming questions from strangers… it turns into a consultancy process that I simply don't have the time for, and as a one-woman farm, my time is extremely valuable to me.

Even as a lifelong gardener and a passionate flower farmer, advertising "garden design services" intimidates me. I don't have a horticultural degree, and have never worked in landscaping. If YOU have a suitable background, offering your expertise to those looking to create gorgeous gardens might make perfect sense. My primary word of advice would be to keep the messaging about your services extremely clear. Are you a consultant or a contractor? Can you take on big jobs? What if someone wants a stone sidewalk, a pond, or a windbreak?

A garden design business could easily overshadow your cut flower dreams, so tread carefully if this is something you'd like to explore.

Workshops

Workshops weren't a huge part of my initial business plan, but about halfway through my first season, I fell completely in love with them. They're such a fun way to share knowledge while also selling your product. If I had to choose between spending a Saturday at a farmer's market, or hosting a workshop on my farm, I would host the workshop, no question.

And what continues to amaze me is that people come out! My farm is between 45 minutes and 1.5 hours away from the closest substantial town or city. The nearest small town is a 15 minute drive, and we're tucked away down several gravel roads that even Google Maps hasn't quite figured out. If you don't have very specific directions, you won't find us.

This remoteness has actually ended up working in our favour. Most of my guests drive in from the cities, some coming from as far as four or five hours away! When people arrive, they feel truly "removed". Our farm is wonderfully peaceful, with plenty of birds and wildlife, and the prairies stretch for miles in every direction. The destination becomes all the more special because of how "off the beaten path" it is.

There are a couple drawbacks, however. In the winter, when the roads are snowy, slippery, and carnival-levels ridiculous, I would never dream of hosting a workshop on my farm. The risk of having to provide several refunds all in one day is too stressful. So I started doing traveling workshops during the festive season, bringing wreath supplies to homes and small businesses that wanted to add a little extra fun to their holiday parties. It worked out wonderfully!

The biggest advantage to hosting workshops is that you're combining your knowledge and your product into a unique, valuable experience for your customers. Rather than spending hours building several wreaths and then worrying they won't sell (and then not selling them for as much as they're actually worth), your customers build the wreaths while learning new skills and enjoying each others' company.

This rings true for flower arrangements, floral crowns, and a wide range of floral crafts. Workshops are the best way to get paid fairly for your time.

There is such a hungry market out there for

experiences. There are so many people who can't do what you're doing, but would be happy to do it for a day!

Another advantage to workshops is this: working a farm is hard and exhausting, and when you're grinding away in the dirt every day, it rarely feels like the dreamy images we see on Instagram. But, workshops allow me to slow down and see all the beauty I've created through my visitors' eyes. My workshop guests truly lifted a veil for me, allowing me to take in and enjoy what I'd created. It was the perfect way to pace out the growing season in a way that regularly reminded me I was building something special.

And if that wasn't enough, workshops are the best way to make money while staying on your farm, without actually having to open your farm to the public. I share the general location of my farm on my website, and after participants have registered, I share directions the week before the workshop date. It gives me more control over who can access my home and private property.

Photoshoots

If you're lucky enough to have a property with established perennials, mature gardens, or cute, rustic outbuildings, those elements can easily be transformed into money makers.

We'll talk about "finding your angle" more in Photography (p.147), but carving out picturesque plots on your farm will pay off in so many ways. Explore your property with a camera, and assess the photogenic potential of every view. Is there a dilapidated farm building with a wall you could plant a garden against? Maybe a vintage rusty vehicle you could fill with sunflowers, or old farming equipment that would work well as a vine trellis. Or maybe you're surrounded by gorgeous wheat fields, a lovely red barn, or a lush tree line. Even an area no bigger than a small city yard can become a beautiful location for photoshoots.

While growing flowers for market often means growing them in standardized, straight lines and cohesive colours, give some thought to the aesthetic potential of your beds and property. I have a flower field where I'm establishing perennials and rotating annuals, but it produces more flowers than I could ever harvest and process in a season. I dry everything I can, and I let plenty go to seed, but I can extend the value of those flowers one step further by opening the field up to photographers.

I also have an outbuilding where I host my floral arrangement workshops, and over time I've discovered the natural light in that building is absolutely stunning. That, paired with the exposed wood beams and flowers everywhere, makes for an ideal space to rent out for wedding and family photo shoots.

Plus, booking photoshoots is another way to earn revenue while keeping your location private. You get to stay on the farm, and the conditions of your guests' visit are clear and scheduled. By allowing photographers to book a shoot on my farm, I can charge $50/hr to $150/hr, and the labour on my part is minimal. I still need to provide Terms and Conditions

Above: Guests building bouquets during one of our summer arrangment workshops.

that clearly communicate what I'm offering (ie: the farm's flowers aren't included unless they're paid for in advance), as well as rules to prevent damage to my plants, but otherwise, it's pretty hassle free.

Events

Speaking of cute outbuildings and picturesque settings, your property could be ideal for hosting events such as farm-to-table dinners, bachelorette parties, weddings, or reunions.

If you're considering hosting such events on your farm, be aware that your farm's insurance requirements could go from "general" to "commercial". You'll also want to take into account any renovation costs in your startup budget; electrical and plumbing upgrades or installations may be required for washroom facilities, a commercial kitchen or bar space, heating, rodent-proofing, and decorative lighting. When I started my farm, I wanted to

convert my large red quonset into a wedding venue, but the renovation costs would have totalled around $50 000. Due to my limited budget, I decided the plan might have to wait. In the meantime, the space works wonderfully for seasonal workshops.

Also keep in mind that every event hosted on your farm will require a certain amount of administrative coordination, and you must clearly specify which of those coordination elements you are willing to take on. If a DIY bride approaches you wanting to have a rustic farm wedding, you could unwittingly find yourself in the position of "wedding planner" unless you've stated clearly from the start that your farm functions solely as a bookable venue (ie: you simply provide the space, brides and event planners must coordinate everything else). Have you ever planned a wedding (other than your own)? It can be extremely time consuming and stressful, especially if you're trying to grow and sell flowers at the same

Above: A gorgeous arrangement created by one of our workshop guests.

time! Event coordination is a full-time job in and of itself, so consider your capacity carefully before offering such services.

And lastly, if you offer food and drinks on your property, you must abide by your government's health and safety regulations. This often requires that food is produced and stored in an approved, commercial-grade kitchen (separate from your household kitchen), and event-based liquor licenses will be required. Speak to your province's or state's liquor agency to confirm what is required for your business.

In terms of food, liquor, and insurance, you could just as easily require that the parties booking your venue find their own certified field caterers, acquire their own day-of liquor license, and secure day-of event insurance (all of which would be reviewed and confirmed by you prior to the event).

Books

If you're someone who loves words, grammar, and typing, writing books can be an extremely satisfying way to spend the quiet off-season. I obviously love writing. I love the rhythm of words and sentences. I love the way a written page can induce flurries of inspiration in the reader's mind. I have a background in critical art writing, and I spent years writing jokes and short screenplays. Words are a joy to me.

Writing a book was also the best way I could think of to address the ever-running stream of questions and inquiries coming through my email and social media, all asking how I run my farm. I was receiving *so* many messages from well-meaning people looking for insights, which was lovely and flattering, but often those single questions merited an entire chapter's worth of responses. I simply didn't have time to sit at my computer each day and write paragraphs and paragraphs of answers to questions, which often led to even more questions. Eventually, I decided to place a very specific value on that time, which is what you paid for this book (thank you!).

I also love books as objects, and enjoy building my tidy little library of hard-copy knowledge. Books don't need batteries, they're easily shareable, but less easy to reproduce (aka: steal). They honour intellectual property and copyrights better than almost every other medium.

But a big fat word of caution: for the self-publisher, they can be very expensive to print and distribute. For my first run of DON'T PANIC, I wrote, edited, formatted, found an affordable printer, and distributed the books all on my own. It was a TON of work, and it was not cheap!! With this current run, once again I've written, edited, and formatted the book, but am distributing it first via Amazon KDP, which lifts a massive chunk of labour and customer service from the overall process, as well as allowing less expensive shipping options (we've been conditioned by large scale distributors to think shipping is cheap, it isn't!!!).

And remember that writing and creating a book is actually only the beginning of *publishing*

a book. You still have to market it, and hopefully sell enough to make back your time and expenses. If you don't have an established following yet, or if you don't have any ideas re: how you will announce your book to the world, this book's Marketing (p.125) and Communications (p.51) sections will help. Marketing your book works the same way as marketing any of your other products!

If you're lucky enough to be approached by a literary publisher, congratulations! You've basically won a literary lottery. Be aware that the timeline for releasing a book through a publisher can be much, much longer (but they pay you to write it!), and some touring may be required to promote the book. I mean, few would say no to such an offer, but the time away from your farm would have to be considered.

Merch

T-shirts, mugs, magnets, aprons, hats, calendars, paperweights, notebooks… anything that can be economically customized and produced on a commercial scale is considered "merch". Merch is different from homemade crafts, in that it's often produced by international companies specializing in mass produced knick knacks.

Because merch typically has a low wholesale cost, it can be a good way to earn a bit of extra income. However, those low costs usually only apply when you're ordering quantities in the hundreds, at least. So you're probably looking at a substantial upfront payment for those cute t-shirts or custom aprons. Can you sell 200 aprons? How many different sizes of t-shirts do you need? If you have to order 50 of each size, that's a hefty upfront investment!

The biggest blunder you can make when it comes to merch, is investing in hundreds of customized doodads that are only relevant for a limited time period. Merch with "Yay Flowers 2020!" printed on it would obviously only have value during the year 2020. A print run of 500 wall calendars will be relevant and sellable for six months, maybe. Maybe you order 500 t-shirts with your logo on them, and then decide to rebrand a year later. Oops!

An alternative to ordering massive amounts of wholesale merch, is to join an online, creator-driven, print-on-demand marketplace like Zazzle, RedBubble, or Society6. By creating a virtual storefront and uploading your designs, you can offer a wide range of t-shirts, mugs, and household items without any upfront investment. Customers order directly from your storefront on the marketplace's website, and you receive a portion of the proceeds Sites like this have worked wonderfully for artists and graphic designers, why not creative flower farmers?.

Whatever products and services you choose to offer, always think about how you can push your plants and flowers further. Think economically. Your farm and capacities are different than anyone else's, but there are plenty of ways to make a sale, whatever sort of flower farm you're planning.

Left and facing page: Merch items created through the artist-merchant platform, Society 6.

Above all, diversify.

If you're hoping to make a profit growing and selling flowers, diversification and adaptability are key, especially if you can't grow flowers year round.

While you don't want to take on too much in your first year, you often won't know how much is "too much" until you've dipped a toe or two into the markets you're most curious about.

And remember, you're the boss! If you start the year targeting florists, and then find it isn't a great fit for you, you're allowed to scale back from that market and change directions anytime. You can try things out without signing contracts, just be sure to respect the people you've made tentative agreements with, and if you must back out, do it as gracefully as possible. And of course, if you decide to change directions, be sure to message it clearly to your customers and supporters.

So what are you good at? Writing? Teaching? Painting? Crafting? Do you have professional skills you could offer to other growers, ie: marketing, graphic design, bookkeeping, or web work? There are endless ways to integrate your unique skill set into your growing business.

Where are you?

My farm is a 10 minute drive from the closest paved road, 15 minutes from the closest small town (which has anemities like a hospital, schools, and grocery store), and 1.5 hours away from two different cities. While I'm slowly working to build a stronger customer base within our local county, cities were my target when I started. A city has higher population density, and markets that will bear better prices for your blooms.

By marketing to cities when I started, my workshops gained momentum much faster, which have allowed me enough breathing room in my cash flow to start targeting my smaller, more local markets too.

If a farmer's market isn't your bag, maybe inquire about street vendor permits in your closest city, and create a small mobile shop near a popular food truck location. Or partner with a florist willing to share retail space, or seek out an artist's cooperative and ask if they have room for flowers.

There are so many options, just make sure your overhead costs don't overwhelm your cash flow before it's had time to get established.

Right: Silver drop eucalyptus.

Left page: Arrangements created for an autumn wedding.

Identifying Your Market

This is the really fun part! Who is going to pay you for all your lovely products and services??

There are SO MANY potential markets for local blooms, the hardest part is picking one (or two! Or three!). Deciding which market to target will depend very much on your scale (as discussed in Production, p.69) and labour capacities (as discussed in Your Team & Allocating Labour, p.172).

For ambitious souls, one fairly significant risk in your early years of growing can be trying to accommodate too many markets at once.

For example: in my first year, I planned to do weddings, CSAs, farmer's markets, upick, workshops, florists... all of it. Weddings seemed like the best way to move beautiful blooms, stretch my artistic muscles, and get a good profit. I created a beautiful, VERY optimistic list of our anticipated flowers for the coming season, and made it available to florists and DIY brides. I was sure we'd have blooms from May to October (ha!). I also sold 30 CSA subscriptions before a single flower had bloomed, agreed to do a farmer's market in the city, offered a "plant rescue" service (thinking it would be a great way to build up the farm), and planned to host workshops and u-pick. It was all perfectly planned, and it all looked GREAT on paper.

Well, our flowers didn't start blooming until mid-July, and because I'd made so many commitments, I spent May and June foraging like a madwoman. Soon our days of working outdoors were stretching from 5am to 8pm, as we hustled to build beds and infrastructure.

Because I had begun marketing the farm in January, by summer we were getting our first exciting media attention, and the queries and requests for our flowers and services were pouring in. The farm had been functional (ie: we were working in the flower beds) for about three months, and opportunities seemed to be opening up on every side of us. Sounds like a good problem to have, right?

I had a meltdown.

Sadly, it's impossible to answer dozens of emails while digging new beds and building infrastructure *you have no idea how to build*, while juggling and managing all other aspects of your new farm. And after working for fifteen hours outside every day, I couldn't handle sifting through emails and private messages until midnight, every day. I crumbled. It was too much.

After a good cry, I made a list identifying every area of stress. Emails were at the top of the list, and hands down, the highest maintenance emails were from brides and florists. The custom needs of each potential order was just too laborious in terms of administration. Too often, these conversations ended with me pulling my hair out, ranting for hours to my farm hand in the field, and eventually having to politely turn down the order. My "plant rescue" service had also blown up and was eating hours of my time for almost no return.

I constantly felt like I was failing. I was running myself ragged, and I needed help.

So I called our first team meeting. At the time, our "team" consisted of me, my farm hand, my mother, and my boyfriend. After expressing myself and hearing their input, the primary issue boiled down to: too many markets. I laid out our various services and market streams, and listened to everyone's feedback re: what our capacity as a group actually was. After some discussion, we decided to nix plant rescue, weddings, and custom orders from the business plan. "For now", we all agreed.

It was a difficult decision, but it saved me. Moving forward from that point, I was able to message our products and services more clearly, and my answer to requests for custom work became, "Maybe next year! Sign up to our newsletter or follow us on social media to stay in the loop!". When someone emails me asking if I could come dig up a cherry tree, I was able to decline without feeling bad about it.

In the following pages, I've identified every market relevant to a new grower that I could think of, along with the pros and cons of each. This list is not definitive, and depending on your area, you may find even more potential sales streams and niches! Just remember that while they're all possible market streams, they might not all be feasible for your scale and capacity in your early years.

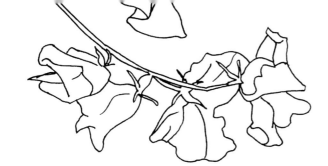

POTENTIAL MARKETS

The Farmer's Market

A farmers' market is a great way to dip a toe into the business of growing blooms for profit. It's one of the best ways to launch your brand through fun displays and face-to-face connections, and markets often don't require vendors to have business licenses, making the whole process of "getting started" a bit simpler. You can utilize a farmers' market as a pick-up point for your CSA members, and they're also great places to meet other farmers and entrepreneurs in your area.

Urban farmers' markets will generally offer higher traffic and better prices for your blooms. An urban market will typically bear prices around $20 to $40 per mixed bouquet. Traffic and higher density doesn't guarantee strong sales, though. In an urban market, tight branding and eye-catching display are especially important, as you're contending with a very busy environment, both visually and economically.

The downside to an urban farmer's market is that table costs are often much higher than their rural counterparts. Unless you're able to jump in on a brand new market, or a market run by a generous community association, table costs could run anywhere from $1000 to $5000 for a season. Be sure to balance those costs against what you'll actually be able to produce and sell.

If your branding, signage and display are innovative, honed, and sure to make an impact, you could simply count those higher table costs towards your marketing budget, and justify the expense in the long term with the exposure the market will provide.

A rural farmers' market still includes the benefits of establishing a simple sales stream, as well as providing an opportunity to showcase your business and display your gorgeous blooms. You get to connect with your local community, and possibly fill a gap in providing fresh blooms to folks who otherwise rely on imported blooms from the local grocery store. That said, a lot more people seem to garden in rural areas, so you may find that rather than purchasing your blooms, people will look at them with appreciation and say "I grow that too!", then walk away. If you plan to target a rural market, focusing on heirloom and less-common varieties might pull more of those flower lovers in, and result in higher sales.

You might also find a rural market can only bear prices around $10 to $20 per mixed bouquet. However those lower prices are often matched with lower table costs, so the balance might still work in your favour.

For both urban and rural farmers' markets, time and labour must be considered. If you're not paying someone to staff your table, you'll be pulled away from your farm for a full day or two, which can be difficult for farming families. Farmers' markets are a LOT of driving, set up, and clean up for one or two days of sales.

Vendor displays must also contend with unpredictable weather, such as summer storms that bring rain, wind, and hail. I've seen vendor's tents and displays completely blown away, products and wares soaked or destroyed, making for downright miserable days of low sales and financial loss. Brutal market days are very hard to stay positive through, and can sometimes break an entire season.

These risks can of course be mitigated through careful planning, and designing your display to withstand any market apocalypse that may befall it.

During the planning stages, take extra time to create something that is well-weighted (tying tents to buckets of sand works!) and wind/rain-proof. You'll also want something that can be set up and taken down in less than half an hour. That way you'll be sitting pretty when other vendors have been literally blown away or are hustling to pack everything up, and better yet, you'll have more time to help them out!

Due to those issues, while farmer's markets are very convenient for customers wishing to support local producers, and they're a great way to make your new farm visible to your customer base, they're actually one of the least sustainable sales streams for farmers. Additionally, many such markets rely on mini-capitalist models of competition. The markets benefit from vendor fees while the vendors duke it out for sales. If another vendor shows up selling flowers, sure, you could potentially become allies, but the fact is *you still really need those sales*.

Any environment that encourages competition over community is bound to create frustration and hard feelings between some vendors. Personally, I'd rather find ways to support and collaborate with other local growers, rather than spend my Saturdays racing them to the bottom.

Florists

In your first year, florists may seem like the most obvious market for your blooms. You grow flowers, they need flowers, easy peasy right?

While supplying florists offers a lot of potential for establishing consistent revenue, these relationships will take time to build. The most significant factor to consider when approaching a florist is that many are accustomed to on-demand, imported wholesale blooms. Imported blooms are highly standardized, particularly when it comes to stem length (18"). They're also often farmed via large scale industrial operations with minimal or exploitative labour laws, and are commonly sprayed with harmful pesticides. You can't, and shouldn't, compete with imported wholesale blooms. An artisan cheese maker does not compete with Cracker Barrel, a local baker does not compete with Wonderbread. Local blooms have value.

Establishing a relationship with a florist will include very clear communication re: the value of your blooms, their seasonality, and your growing methods. You're allowed to take the lead when it comes to setting prices. If a florist isn't interested, simply move on and find one who is. There are many florists joining the "slow flower" movement and embracing seasonal design who would be happy to support you.

There are a couple different ways to approach a florist. You could pop in with a "sample bucket" and a basic (but professional looking) info sheet listing what you're growing and what your farm is all about. Then simply introduce yourself quickly and leave your card, letting them know they can contact you with more questions. Or, you can send an introductory email inviting them to your farm, or inquiring if they'd be interested in fresh local blooms. Be sure to include an image of yourself holding your lovely blooms in your email's signature, so they connect with your face.

Once your business starts building momentum, you may find that florists start coming to you. Be sure to communicate clearly from the start what you're able to provide, and what your ordering processes are. In your first year, I advise against taking special orders more than a couple weeks in advance, as a sudden storm could potentially wipe out that anticipated crop, which would create a stressful situation both for you and the florist.

And if you find a wonderful florist who loves your flowers and happily pays you fair prices for them, hang onto them! Do not bend over backwards to appease a demanding or disrespectful florist. Contrary to popular assumptions, you do not exist to serve florists. Your business does not bow to theirs. There are so many ways to sell your flowers, why settle for a relationship that doesn't work for

you?

CSA Subscriptions

CSA stands for "Community Supported Agriculture" or "Community Shared Agriculture." Exact definitions may vary slightly from region to region, but its purpose is consistent throughout the market farming industry. Alberta Agriculture and Forestry defines it accordingly:

"Community Supported Agriculture or Community Shared Agriculture (CSA) is a community of individuals or families who support a chosen farm and its family. Each individual or family purchases, in advance, a share, called a subscription, of the year's crop. Thus, the customers become virtual partners or 'co-producers' in the farm, sharing risk and reward with the farm family. Throughout the growing season, each week subscribing member receives equal shares of the freshly harvested food from the farmer."

CSAs are a great way to pull in early sales, ideally helping to cover your early season costs. I've sold bouquet subscription CSAs as Christmas "stocking stuffers" (subscribing customers for the following summer), as late winter "reprieve sales", and as midsummer "flash sales". If you have the capacity to supply and distribute the flowers, CSA subscriptions are a great way to make sales and build your customer base.

In my first year, I offered five month "one bouquet a week" subscriptions, thinking I would have flowers from May to October. LOL! I was grossly optimistic, and that season kicked my butt. I sold 30 subscriptions before I'd grown any flowers, and while I would never, ever commit to such a long subscription again, those CSA members are a huge reason why my farm got the initial boost it did.

Your CSA members aren't just a source of sweet spring revenue, they're your cheering squad. Your elite force of marketing missionaries. If treated well, these lovely folks, who purchased CSAs specifically to support your business, are one of your most valuable marketing assets.

You MUST treat this lovely group as well as you can. Your CSA subscriptions should include benefits for your members that no one else will receive. Create an email distribution list that is exclusively CSA members (be sure to BCC if it's via email though!), and send special offers to them first. Offer incentives to renewing annual memberships, such as discounts on workshops or next year's subscriptions. Acknowledge and thank them frequently online and in your messaging. Let everyone know this sweet group of supportive folks is just the coolest little club, and regularly tell them why!

If you reach your annual CSA cap in the spring (and you should definitely set a cap! In our first year we did 30 5-month subscriptions, plus 10 more "flash" subscriptions in the summer, and it was a LOT for us), offer a waiting list. Waiting lists not only give an air of exclusivity to your subscriptions, but more importantly, they're a really easy way to reach your eager spring supporters next year!

When your CSA Members feel taken care of, they will tell everyone who will listen about your flowers.

Currently, my farm offers two 5 week subscriptions; one "early summer", from mid July to mid August, and one "late summer", from mid August to mid September. They are one bouquet per week, picked up during set time frames at a predetermined location, or delivered for an extra fee ($10 per week, or $50 for the entire subscription). The early summer subscription is $100 CAD plus tax, and the late summer subscription is $125 CAD plus tax. The bouquets are about 20 stems each, and are a mix of whatever is seasonal. Their value works out to about $20 per bouquet, which is a great deal for fresh local flowers! This value is a selling point I emphasize to encourage people to sign up early.

The biggest "con" for CSAs is, if you aren't organized, with clear terms of service and a streamlined transaction process, they can easily become a logistical nightmare. These details MUST be worked out well in advance, before you announce your subscriptions. I don't allow custom requests, I don't offer credit for missed pickups, and I don't allow switching between pick up and delivery. Peak season, I'm just too darn busy for random personalized services. Draw your boundaries early on, to save yourself many peak season headaches.

Another small "con" is that, while the sales feel GREAT early in the year, if you get overambitious and sell too many, handling those subscriptions during peak season could eat up all your summer farming time. If you still need to pull in revenue while your blooms are bursting, fulfilling 80 CSA subscriptions will consume a ton of your energy, and will make it difficult to supply your other markets.

Also, consider the labour creating bouquets requires. When you're just learning how to build bouquets, making 20 mixes could easily take all afternoon. Honing your bouquet making process is critical for efficient time management. It now takes me about two hours to build 40 bouquets, and that's still too long. I'm working towards 100 bouquets in an hour (this would require a helper!). Floret offers a wonderful video tutorial on speedy bouquet building, it's a "must view" for anyone marketing mixed bouquets.

And I remind my members frequently that their subscription's primary purpose is to support our farm. Our subscriptions are not just cheap flowers! Signing up includes sharing seasonal risk. If a storm were to wipe out all of our flowers, our members would not get refunds, because their dollars were meant to help us in such cases. Always keep your farm, your story, and the realness of your business close to the surface while marketing your subscriptions.

Above: Zinnias, considered a workhorse by many flower farmers..

Farm Stand

A farm stand can be a very convenient way for market farmers to move their product. A cute little stall at the end of the driveway, quaint signage, an "honour system" cash box, no staff, no driving… sounds ideal right?

I've had several people tell me I should consider this option, but for me, there's one huge catch: within a 24 timeframe, maaaybe two cars drive past our farm. We have absolutely zero traffic. And I actually love how remote our farm is! I'm a very private person, that's why I moved to a farm! I don't want to broadcast our location. I don't want random visitors wandering through my gardens. And I especially don't want to make our property or my family vulnerable to crime. So, with no traffic, and no desire to make our location public, a farm stand isn't a great option for me.

Another "con" is potential theft. A cash box sitting unsupervised, or even bolted to the stand, could easily attract the wrong attention. And the honour system only works if you live in an "honourable" location. A small community that looks out for each other would probably work great for a farm stand. A driveway next to a major city? Maybe not.

And finally, you likely won't get the best return for your blooms. A farm stand bouquet might be priced between $10 to $15. That's a steal for fresh flowers! Are you making any profit on those blooms? Remember, if you're doing this as a business, you need to pull in revenue. If you're more interested in casual sales as a hobby gardener, you're welcome to price your flowers however you choose, but keep in mind you might be undercutting other flower farmers in the area who *do* rely on flower sales to feed their families.

Grocery Stores

Grocery stores are a potentially excellent way to move plenty of blooms and secure seasonal revenue. If you have at least one year of growing for profit under your belt, and can estimate your seasonal yields with a relatively high amount of certainty, a good relationship with a grocery store could spell success for your small business. For myself, there are a couple essential pieces to consider before stepping into an agreement with a grocery store:

Pricing. As we discussed in Pricing Your Flowers (p.78), you will have to decide what prices are going to work best for you in terms of making a legitimate return on all your hard work. When dealing with grocery stores, you'll be working within wholesale pricing, but before you settle on those prices, do some research into that particular store's target demographic. Are they specialty/boutique? Are they rural? Are they a superchain looking to source locally? Whatever scale they are, you should have some sense of their prices and customers before entering into talks with them. Visit the location. Ask your network if anyone shops there. Scope out any other florals they sell. Are the flowers in good shape? Do they rotate them out when the blooms fade? This shop could potentially be representing your farm. Lovely, fresh displays will make you look very good, but rows of sad, wilted bouquets won't help you in terms of building your customer base.

Capacity. How many bouquets will they want per week? Can you feasibly add 20 bouquets per week to your seasonal bouquet-making schedule? 40? 80? When will you have flowers available? Do you offer any alternatives to fresh flowers during the off season, such as holiday wreaths or dried bouquets? How will you price them?

Distribution. How far away are they? How many bouquets will you be delivering to them, and how often? Do you have a vehicle that can accommodate that capacity?

Contracts. This is a big one. One the one hand, having a contract that clarifies your agreement and secures seasonal revenue is great. You get partial or full funds upfront, which could help with your tight cashflow in the spring. These pluses alone justify the wholesale trade off. However, what if a storm wipes out your farm mid season? What if you overestimate your yields and are caught short? What if it's just you building all those bouquets, and you can't keep up? What if you get sick or injured? A contract, with all its security, can also make life much harder if things don't go as planned.

Before entering into a contract with a grocer, be sure you've carefully weighed all these pieces. Never step into a contract agreement blindly. Always, always do your research.

Restaurants, Hotels, Showhomes

Many restaurants, hotels and showrooms use fresh flowers throughout their spaces, and many pay florists top dollar for that steady supply. Sending out brochures or making contact via email early in the year could lead to some lucrative relationships for your farm.

In these instances, you may end up playing the role of "farmer florist", so be prepared for questions around design, colour palettes, and flower varieties. If your growing season is limited, and you don't plan to supplement with imported flowers during the off season, you must state that fact during initial talks. If a hotel is "all about roses", and you don't grow roses, you probably won't be able to accommodate them.

Approach these potential relationships as clearly and professionally as you can. They will want to see examples of your work, they will want clear pricing and some sense of the flowers you offer, and the customer service elements may increase as you edge closer into florist territory.

Wholesale Suppliers

The same companies that distribute imported blooms could very well be interested in purchasing your local flowers. The most important factor to consider here is the sheer scale that these wholesalers operate on. Thousands of blooms rotate through their doors on a daily basis. Are you looking to move a few pails of blooms, or are you planning to grow a full acre of cash crops? Most importantly, remember that whatever you're thinking of selling, you'll be selling to wholesalers for less than wholesale prices.

For small scale growers, selling your flowers for wholesale prices directly to grocery stores and florists is already a stretch for your bottom line. You don't have dozens of acres, or massive mechanical harvesting equipment, you're a market farm. Your labour costs are high, and you're focused on maximizing productivity within your small plot. You can't afford to sell your flowers at .50 cents or less per stem.

If you're thinking, "well, a sale's a sale!", I'm here to tell you no, it isn't. A bad sale is a bad sale. A bad sale undercuts the value of your product, it steals away the value of your labour, and, if a bad sale turns into many bad sales (her flowers are SO CHEAP!) it will eventually sink your business. Unless you have a glorious acre of procut sunflowers blooming throughout the season with nowhere else to go, or several acres of peonies that need to be moved quickly in bulk numbers, selling to wholesale suppliers might not be for you.

DIY Brides

I'm not going to sidestep around this: brides are hard. They are where all the trickiest pieces of customer service collide: a high pressure, milestone event. Perishable, seasonal product that the customer knows almost nothing about. Bargain hunting. #Instagram expectations. Amateur event planning.

Above: An arrangement of colourful summer blooms including dahlias, asters, didiscus, craspedia, delphinium, laceflower, eucalyptus, and sweet peas.

Mothers...
We discussed floristry under Floral Design Services (p.93), and certainly, all those elements apply when it comes to many brides. However, as Pinterest and Instagram inspire countless couples to get thrifty and creative while planning their big day, DIY brides not only want the cutest flowers out there, but also the *cheapest*. This trend directs many brides towards flower farms. Do they want to "support local", or do they want cheap flowers? Before you enter into any talks with a DIY bride, make sure they're coming to you for the right reason!

Once you start attracting brides who value your work, you must have processes in place that won't burn you out after the first transaction. Think of your DIY brides as beautiful wild horses, who also happen to be coordinating the biggest event of their lives. They need SPACE. Gentle guidance. Appreciate their passion and energy, but always from a safe distance. In herds, they can be overwhelming; breathless, half-composed query emails; questions with no reference points (ie: no subject line and one sentence: "hi how many flowers can I get for my tables?"); an odd inability to read website pages or reply emails...

Above all, DIY brides need clear processes. The more reading you can get them to do re: your services, *before* you start discussing wedding details, the better. I almost always answer initial wedding queries by sending them straight to my "Weddings" page on my website. I spent a LOT of time thinking through my services, my processes, and my capacity for weddings. All of that information is laid out very clearly on my website, so I don't have to explain it over and over again.

Once a bride has read through the information on my website, they're invited to submit a query form, which covers all the details of what they're looking for, essentially corralling their expectations via reminders and clarifications throughout the form. When a form submission shows up in my inbox, I know they have read through all the info, and have a much firmer grasp of my services than a random inquiry would.

Additionally, I have a very clear "Mutual Respect Policy" on my website, that is also included in my confirmation contracts. If any customer, bride or no, treats me or my staff/family disrespectfully, I reserve the right to cancel their order without refund. I'm a farmer before anything else, and as such I have absolutely no time for entitlement or tantrums. Any client I take on is fully aware of that, and consequently, almost all of my customer interactions are lovely and respectful.

Flower Truck or Trailer

I'm sure you've seen one: an adorable VW van converted to a mobile flower shop, a sweet vintage pickup truck with a canopy installed in the back, or something like my farm's little horse trailer turned pop up flower shop. These vehicles are ADORABLE. They turn heads and cause people to involuntarily whip out their phones for insta photos. There are certainly pros and cons to these cuties though, which are extremely important to consider before jumping in and buying the first darling rickshaw you see.

Storage capacity. Ideally, you'll want your unit to be a self contained mini floral shop, right? That will include storage space for all your flowers inside. Whether this space also doubles as cargo capacity, aka storage space that can safely hold your flowers during transit, must be considered as well.

We divided our horse trailer in half and used one side for storage, one for sales. It worked great! The storage side is insulated, and I briefly considered installing a generator-powered air conditioner in it, but we didn't end up needing one. We don't get too many summer scorchers in my area, and as long as the flowers are shaded and hydrated, the trailer works just fine for one-day sales.

If you plan on transporting flowers in your truck or trailer, remember to install racks that will prevent buckets from tipping and sliding. And generally, trailers are MUCH bumpier rides than trucks. In a trailer, a small bump on the highway could potentially send all your beautiful blooms flying, and a mess of petals, stems and water isn't something you want to deal with when arriving at your destination! It isn't impossible to transport flowers in a trailer, but definitely remember to drive carefully with your precious cargo.

Display. If you're modifying a vehicle, it's likely your road laws won't allow DIY installations of rods and racks sticking out every which way on the exterior of your rig, as they would be a serious liability to other drivers and pedestrians. However, a bright, inviting exterior display of your flowers is essential for

Left: Our horse trailer converted into a mini flower market. This trailer has become the flagship of my business, and works wonderfully as a marketing tool.

pulling customers over to you, and you want your rig to be insta post worthy too! So how do you create a beautiful, convenient display?

First off, you'll need a metal worker. For trailers, there isn't too much risk in devaluing the vehicle as a whole with DIY modifications, so a hobby blacksmith or casual auto mechanic could easily become your best friend. For a truck or van, you're going to want the modifications to be less... permanent. A lot of "aftermarket" custom modifications can devalue your vehicle, or make it illegal to drive on public roadways. This can be a tricky, and expensive, problem to solve.

For motor vehicles like a truck or a van, professional paint jobs and auto decals are the safest options. If the vehicle was a pile of junk to start with, a careful, DIY paint job using auto rustproof paint is certainly an option, and adding a few sturdy, nonintrusive

hooks to hang display racks from is definitely a possibility too. Just be sure you've done your research, and don't accidentally add anything that will result in tickets or fines.

And remember, any exterior displays will need shade! We installed a removable, adjustable market umbrella on ours, but there are lots of options for mobile canopies!

Expense. Modifying a motor vehicle is not cheap, and neither is maintaining one. For myself, I chose a trailer over a truck, because while I still needed a truck to haul the trailer, I could then unhitch that truck and continue using it for farm and family errands. The trailer was a low upfront cost, was relatively cheap to modify, and when not in use, there's nothing mechanical to maintain. We check the tires regularly, and make sure mice aren't turning it into a condo complex in the winter, but otherwise the initial investment and maintenance costs are minimal compared to a vehicle. And if I decide to close my business? I'd turn it into a chicken coop, and have very few "sunken" costs to worry about.

Primarily, flower trucks and trailers are great marketing tools. If your main sales stream is a farmer's market, a farm stand, or if you plan to move your shop from spot to spot frequently, they can be extremely efficient sales tools. Just be sure to consider the labour and expense they could potentially consume.

Retail (Brick and Mortar)

Brick and mortar shops have an irresistible pull to new entrepreneurs. The idea of running a cute little storefront in a nice part of town has been drilled into our small business brains since the time most of us first envisioned running a business. We imagine the signage, the decor, the renovations, cool lighting and unique furniture... fill that space with flowers and it's all an absolute dream!

But oh my god, what a financial risk they are. On top of your new market farming business, signing a lease for a retail location increases your risk of failure by at least double. There are so many factors that could easily tank your flowery dreams: location, landlords, renovations, neighbourhood demographics, population density, walkability, parking, but most importantly: RENT. Most locations require you sign a yearly lease, which means no breaks for off-season slowness. Retail locations also require staff (you still have to farm, remember?), property taxes, utilities,

separate licenses and insurance, and all the facilities required for keeping flowers in good shape, ie: a walk in cooler, air conditioning, a distribution vehicle, a bucket washing station, bouquet processing tables, etc. And you'll need someone to MANAGE all those elements on a daily basis, as you manage your farm.

If you really want to set up in a shop, my main advice is this: you will need a large enough financial cushion to cover a full year of "worst case scenario" operations. Whatever your projections for the business are, assume you'll only make 20% of that in your first year, and plan from there. In today's volatile economy, "setting up shop" in a retail location is one of the most expensive and risky endeavours a new business owner can take on.

Alternately, you can turn your gardens and your farm into a lovely, flowery experience for customers wishing to purchase fresh flowers and genuinely support their local producers! Make your property or plot work for you. A flower farm carries so much more intrigue than just another shop! It's a lifestyle, a dream, and an extremely beneficial addition to its rural economies. There's so much more story to tell when it comes to a flower farm. Embrace that!

On-Farm Sales

Aside from a farm stand, there are a lot of other ways you can market and sell flowers directly from your farm. Workshops, which we discuss on p.95, are a great way to move flowers and make a good return on your time.

If you don't mind frequent visitors, you could also just set business hours and make your location public, allowing people to come by and purchase flowers during set hours.

As I've noted several times throughout this book, I've been very hesitant to make our farm's location public. Because our farm is our home, and because we have such a small team, there are just too many risks to consider. Our security aside, our weeks are also extremely busy, and "time off" comes along rarely and unexpectedly. If I decide to take a bit of downtime due to a rainy afternoon, illness, exhaustion, or if I somehow run out of work (this never happens lol!), you better believe the last thing I want is a stranger wandering into my yard, expecting a tour!

Beyond that, making your location public could mean plenty of visitors, but it won't guarantee sales. And nothing, *nothing*, is more frustrating than spending an hour answering a random visitor's questions, and then watching them snap a couple pics and leave without buying anything. Your time has value.

The best solution to random wanderers and people who are just visiting to decorate their Instagram feeds, is to make visits by appointment only. Once a potential customer has contacted you, stated their intentions, and set a time to visit, then you can share your location with them.

I go one step further and require a $50 spending minimum (about one bucket of

flowers), which is payable upon confirmation of their appointment, before they arrive at the farm. Visitors are expected to be punctual, and their visit must be limited to about 15 minutes. They select flowers from our pre-harvested blooms in the cooler or studio space, fill their bucket, pay for any stems over their $50 pre-payment, and then off they go! They can ask for permission to take photos afterwards, provided they don't enter any of the gardens. All told, it's a nice visit for them, and a good sale for me.

U-Pick

I've separated "U-Pick" from "On-Farm Sales" because while u-pick would certainly happen on your farm, there are several elements of this service that should be considered before advertising it. If certain factors aren't weighed, your guests will end up taking home a lot of blooms that will end up wilting prematurely, which may result in poor reviews of your flowers.

Harvest windows. Most flowers, with the exception of zinnias, yarrow, and precious few others, are best harvested before 8am or after 9pm, during the coolest parts of the day when the plants are full of energy. Do you really want to be hosting guests before 8am, and would enough people actually come out that early to make it worth your while?

Likewise, at the end of your day, when the sun is setting and your body is powering down, do

Above: Lavender asters. Asters are a late season flower for us, but are well worth the wait.

you really want to switch "on" again to host u-pickers? And of course, do you really want to answer the steady stream of "why didn't my flowers last?" if customers are harvesting them midday? If you have a group of keener seniors who are up at the crack of dawn looking for a party, by all means, set up some u-pick fun for them! Otherwise, it may be tricky to accommodate people while also ensuring your flowers perform well.

Training. Over and over and over again, you will have to train your guests on best harvesting and conditioning practices. If someone shows up with a pair of dirty craft scissors, their flowers will suffer. If someone assumes they can just pluck the flowers with their hands, like a princess in a fairy meadow, their flowers will suffer. If someone harvests a gorgeous bouquet but then doesn't put them in water

right away, their flowers will suffer. This is where it won't be enough to say "you pick them, they're your responsibility!", because you want your flowers to SHINE and pull in more business. Are you able to provide clean snips and water buckets to every guest, and walk them through a harvest and conditioning tutorial at the beginning of each session? This is starting to sound more like a workshop, which you could probably earn a much better return on!

Damage. Even guests with the best intentions will accidentally step backwards onto plants, or break a stalk as they walk past, or pop a bloom off a stem and toss it, assuming it "didn't count". Many of my visitors have crushed or snapped plants that were due to bloom later in the season, simply because they assumed they were just lumps of green.

When you put all of your emotional and physical energy into your plants, it's really, really hard to watch them get carelessly smashed. Toss children into the equation, and my god, you've got a disastrous loss just waiting to happen. But, you can't babysit every customer, and you can't sour their experience by yelling "CAREFUL, THOSE ARE IMPORTANT" every five seconds...

Some growers create gardens specifically for u-pick customers, filled with hardy, prolific bloomers that bounce back readily. Personally, once I considered the reality of u-pick, I decided it was just more work than the returns could justify.

Online Sales

If you have healthy online engagement and know your audience well enough, you could potentially skip having a sales location altogether, and choose to sell exclusively through an online shop. This would take some technical website know how, but platforms such as Wix offer streamlined ecommerce services that make this option feasible and affordable.

For my own farm, I set up online sales much like a regular e-shop. During the growing season, different flower varieties are listed as "products", and detailed descriptions are included with each product. Before customers purchase their flowers, I emphasize that they must contact me to set up a pick up time. Then, the transaction happens via the website.

If you have someone able to deliver, you could simply have customers enter their address, along with a preferred delivery window. There are several florists who offer similar services, but you have the advantage of farm fresh product! With tight messaging that includes the story of your farm and your flowers, you could easily shine as the more appealing option. You could also market this shop directly to florists, setting prices at wholesale rates and making the shop a member's only space.

Before you start building your flashy web store though, do some research to see if there's already a service in place for local growers. If a co-op or collective of growers has formed in your area, it may be that they're also consolidating their sales services. Do some digging!

If you're American, you can start with Rooted Farmers. This is an online service that connects growers with florists, taking a hefty load of administration off the plate of the grower. This service is new as of 2020, but may expand through Canada and the UK in the coming seasons.

If a service doesn't exist in your area yet, it may be worthwhile to connect with other local growers and create one! Shared efforts are always beneficial, not only because they lighten your workload, but because they connect you with a wonderful community in the process.

*Chinese forget-me-nots. These are a lovely, true blue flower that
adds dainty whimsy to any bouquet or arrangement.*

FRESH
Flowers

❀ ALBERTA GROWN
❀ BOUQUETS & BUNCHES ❀

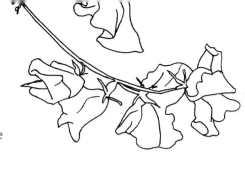
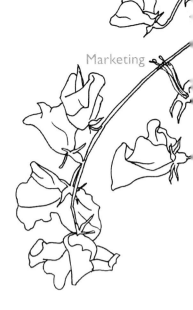

Left: All of your signage should be legible from a distance. Give the typefonts you use special consideration, as they can go a long way in terms of drawing eyes towards you!

Marketing

So you know *what* you're selling and *where* you want to sell. Now *who* are you selling to, and *how* do you reach them? As we discussed in Branding & Key Messaging (p.41), the first step to reaching your target markets is identifying them in your messaging. If you've decided to do u-pick, your customers need to know! If you want to woo florists, address them directly in your messaging and dangle those dinner plate dahlias like bait! Likewise, if you're hosting workshops, selling at a market, or selling CSAs. Let them know you're ready for them!

Starting out, the first few steps of reaching your market often feel awkward, and it takes time to establish a confident voice with an effective strategy. For many businesses, marketing is an expensive endeavour which requires a hefty budget.

Luckily for you, you have several advantages when it comes to marketing your product:

1. Your flowers are beautiful.

2. During times of global anxiety, your blooms and gardens are a welcome respite.

3. You're pursuing a romanticized dream shared by many.

4. You GROW LOCAL, which is increasingly appealing to conscientious consumers.

IDENTIFYING YOUR DEMOGRAPHICS

Okay so first, WHO do you want to tell about your business? Addressing your market in your messaging is one thing, but really, who are you inviting along on this journey?

Forget analytics. Envision an audience of smiling faces ready to hear about your business. Who are they?

The first demographic you should recognize is YOU. Your age, your cultural and social perspectives, and your interests. As unique as each of us are, there are actually THOUSANDS of potential friends out there who are just like us. They share our dreams, our anxieties, and are drawn to like-minded souls. They'll find you if your messaging is genuine and true to your vision.

And outside of YOU, there are many more not exactly like you, who will still be keen to support you. Do you love your mom? Then you'll probably love a lot of other moms too. Do you love your dad? Make all the other dads proud. Do you have a strong affinity for the horticultural community? Include horticultural tips in your posts! Are you a lifelong gardener? A total newbie? A florist? A parent? Do you come from a long line of farmers? Are you a former urbanite? A backyard farmer?

Identify who YOU are as a demographic, who YOUR circles of support are, and then work from there. Reach out the way YOU would expect to be reached out to.

4,427 Followers

Above: I feel very fortunate to have the audience I do. I review my followers regularly to get a sense of who they are and how my business might serve them better.

Above: A late season harvest of asters.

REACHING YOUR DEMOGRAPHICS

The best, most tried and true methods for reaching your target markets are:

Your Website

Creating a website can feel like an incredibly daunting task for anyone unfamiliar with the process. Only a few years ago, it was nearly impossible to get a professional and functional website without hiring a designer and spending upwards of $20,000. Those times are far behind us now, as DIY web building platforms get more and more user friendly, and are vastly less expensive.

Whether you decide to launch a website right away, or want to wait and feel things out first, as soon as you decide you're ready to reach your public, you should have one.

"But do I *need* a website?"

As daunting as it may seem, yes. Your website is your online home base, a landing pad for customers, media, and anyone else who wants a more fulsome look at what your business is all about. It's also a place you can claim as *yours*, breaking away from social media homogeny and presenting your business in all its unique and wonderful glory. And if a social media platform were to glitch or crash, you wouldn't lose your ability to do business along with it.

It also reflects professionalism within the industry, and is a critical tool in streamlining inquiries, orders, workshop registration, and maintaining newsletters. Think of your website as the online "head" of your business, and social media platforms as your online "arms and legs". Social media can't offer all the same functionalities and organizational capacities, but it's very useful for redirecting customers to your website to do real business.

".COM or .CA (or .AU/.UK etc)?"

Buy both ".com" and your own country's domain code if you can! You can link both domains to the same website, and it prevents confusion should anyone else decide to start a business with the same name.

".com" is also best for your SEO (Search Engine Optimization) results, as customers are more likely to search ".com" than ".ca" (or another country code). You'll get more traffic to your website overall if you register both domains, and connect both to your website. If someone has the ".com" version of your business name, I'd advise you to consider a new name altogether, rather than registering the ".ca" version. In terms of online marketing and communications, it just keeps things much more clear. ".com" is wired into our brains when it comes to searching websites, so make sure customers are landing on YOUR site, rather than someone else's.

"*When* do I need a website?"

It's up to you, but a website will benefit your business the moment it's published, whatever stage your business is at. It can be as simple as a single home page with basic information about your products and how to contact you, or it can be a multi-page, dynamic informational experience for potential customers and supporters.

Additionally, buying your website domain as soon as you've committed to your business name will effectively "save your spot" online. You don't even have to publish your website right away, just reserve the domain as soon as you know you'll need it. New businesses are born every second, grab that sweet domain while you can!

Help our farm

Subscribe to our Newsletter
Stay in the loop! News, sales, and all the flower fun.

👤 Name

✉ Email Address

Subscribe Now

© 2020 Alberta Girl Acres

Contact Us

The key components your website should have are:

- Information about you and your flower business.

- Products and services you provide and who they're for.

- A contact page or a contact form on your home page.

The main advantage to building your own, aside from how much cheaper it is than having a professional do it, is that edits and updates can be made exactly when and how you want them to be. No waiting for the "web guy" to get back to you, no missing key timeframes or promotional windows because of technical delays, and no added expense of paying someone for what are often very simple changes. Keep it simple, and your online processes and updates will stay simpler later on.

And of course, if you're still completely lost, reach out to your personal network. It's likely someone you know is familiar with Wix, Wordpress, Squarespace, or a similar platform, and would be happy to help you out.

Remember, you have product to barter with too! Maybe trade a basic website for a CSA subscription?

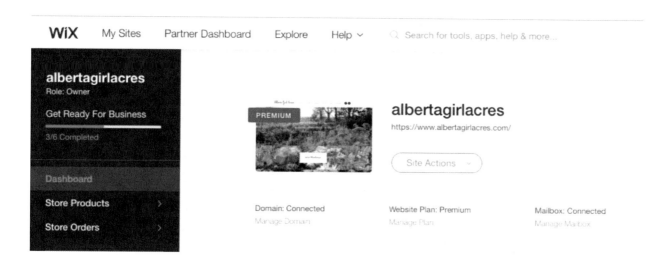

Social Media

This is perhaps the most effective, FREE online marketing tool there is. Once you have your website, branding and messaging in place, it's simply a matter of opening an account and plugging everything in!

Are some social media platforms better than others? Absolutely. And which platforms you choose to use can depend highly on which demographic you want to target.

Instagram
For the purposes of a cut flower business, you can't beat Instagram. It's truly where the industry thrives, and is probably responsible for the upsurgence of cut flower farming overall.

Facebook
Second to that, Facebook can be easily linked to your Instagram, and will reach small business owners, office culture, stay-at-home and work-at-home folks, and others (primarily Gen Xers and Baby Boomers).

Pinterest
Pinterest is where you'll reach brides, daydreamers, and event professionals.

Twitter
Twitter has, for the most part, become flooded with toxicity and political punditry, and I would not recommend it for a cut flower business.

Many farmers find satisfaction in **blogging** as well, which can be a great way to stay connected to your supporters.

Don't stress about maintaining a presence on every platform, or keeping up with all the new trends. Conserve your energy by focusing on one or two platforms while getting your early years off the ground.

Remember: you are selling a dream as much as you are selling flowers. Let your social media accounts reflect that dream! And most importantly, enjoy what you're posting! I often use my feed as a reminder that all our hard work is actually creating a ton of beauty. Sometimes YOU need to see your dream as much as your followers do!

SOCIAL MEDIA DO'S

DO
Create business accounts separate from your personal accounts.

DO
Link your business' Instagram and Facebook page for more convenient posting.

DO
Include your website and *general* location in your profile.

DO
Search similar business names on social media during the planning stages, to avoid being confused with someone else.

DO
Make your @handle your business name.

DO
Keep you @handles consistent throughout your various social media accounts.

DO
Include a photo of yourself holding your blooms as your profile picture. You'll experience better quality engagement if people can see your face.

DO
Space out your captions in paragraphs, dividing them with periods, dashes, or emoticons, in order to ease legibility. Include hashtags at the bottom of each post.

DO
Keep the glamour in your main feed. Many growers share the less glamourous aspects of their farms in their stories, which works well for "behind the scenes" peeks.

DO
Be honest and genuine in your posts. Let your followers hear your voice and get a sense of who you are.

DO
Keep yours and your family's safety and privacy in mind at all times.

DO
Tag and give credit to other small businesses or kind souls who have helped you out in any way, but DO ask for permission before tagging them, or posting their faces online.

DO
Include your social media handles on your day-to-day market signage.

DO
Redirect customer inquiries to your website or email address, for ease of organization.

DO
Remember people are following your account as a reprieve from the noise of social media. Keep it light as often as you can!

SOCIAL MEDIA **DON'TS**

DON'T
Publish your exact address unless you are regularly open to the public, or have the staff capacity to accommodate random strangers.

DON'T
Publish your personal phone number online, unless you want to be interrupted constantly by random inquiries and spam calls.

DON'T
Cram hashtags into the main captions of your posts. It #disjoints the reader's #experience and makes you sound #robotic and #impersonal.

DON'T
Go on a following spree in the hopes of gaining more followers. You will saturate your feed with irrelevant content, which will dilute the usefulness of the platform. It's also bad optics for a business to be following 2000 people when it only has 300 followers.

DON'T
Take it personally if your heroes don't follow you back. They are extremely busy and likely get many requests per day. Requesting a follow back is also bad ettiquitte, as each business owner has their own online rules, and it puts them in an awkward position.

DON'T
Ever respond to trolls. It will never, ever be worth your time, and will only consume valuable energy. Ignore, block, rinse, repeat.

DON'T
Ever smacktalk another industry person online. The degrees of separation are fewer than you think, and you'll only create a bad name for yourself.

DON'T
Use or post images that are not yours without either asking permission, or crediting/tagging their source.

DON'T
Go crazy with filters. Sometimes using photo editing tools is necessary, but heavily filtered photos look tacky. Especially when your blooms are already so beautiful!

DON'T
Post on your main timeline every five minutes, or more than three times per day. Ongoing updates are great for "stories", but your main feed should be uncluttered and consistent.

DON'T
Indulge in oversharing your personal woes, or at least, do it very very rarely. You may regret giving strangers access to yourself later on, and your business shouldn't suffer for online meltdowns.

DON'T
Complain or post about low engagement. It won't help and will only turn people off to your content.

#smallbusiness #marketfarming #marketgardening
#smallscalefarming #flowerfarming #flowerbusiness
#sustainablebusiness #farmingforprofit #workshop
#businessplanning #farmmanagement
#businessmanagement

Making Hashtags Work For You

A lot of people are confused by hashtags. What's the point of putting a little # before a couple words? Do you just make up your own? How do you know which ones are the good ones?

Think of hashtags as breadcrumbs. Users of social media often search hashtags to find content that interests them, so leaving a breadcrumb trail for them makes it much easier for them to find your content. For example: if you want to pull lovers of flower farms to your business, you would use the hashtag #flowerfarm. If you're a Canadian flower farmer, you could use the hashtags #Canadian #flowerfarmer, and those searching for Canadian flower farms will have a much easier time finding you.

Many people also follow hashtags, so they can see every bit of content that appears using that hashtag. I follow #seasonalfloweralliance, a hashtag started by Floret Farm, and without fail, it shows me gorgeous posts by flower farmers committed to growing seasonal blooms. It helps me discover new farms to follow, and also gives me a great look at who is growing what, all over the world.

You can also create hashtags as a way to help your followers find content specific to your farm only. If you take regular photos of yourself holding big bundles of blooms, creating a hashtag for such posts will allow your followers to tap the tag, then find every photo you've ever posted of you holding your blooms. For example, #Laurasbloombabies or #armfullofflowersAB. It can really be whatever you want, as long as it signifies what your followers will find should they follow the "breadcrumb" trail. Make these hashtags intentional, and don't crowd the post with more than are absolutely necessary.

Using hashtags can also be compared to casting a net to pull in new followers; there are ways to cast wider nets, such as using singular hashtags rather than plural hashtags (ie: #flowerfarm vs #flowerfarms). As you type in your hashtag, suggestions will often automatically generate, and you'll notice which version is used more widely (usually the singular version). Wider usage means casting a wider net. Another example of this is using non-geo-specific hashtags like #flowerfarm over #albertaflowerfarm.

Above: When the farm is quiet, take time to reevaluate your products and services, but stay in touch with your audience.

Off-Season Posting

Tossing glorious blooms into your feed throughout the growing season is fun and easy, and with minimal effort you'll find yourself swimming in "oohs" and "aaahs" in the form of likes, comments, and new followers. But for colder climate growers, what happens when the season ends? How do you maintain that engagement and keep your followers' interest throughout the winter?

This is where a social media strategy comes in handy. Your strategy doesn't have to be complicated, and can be as simple as a short list pinned on your office wall. It can include simple rules like "dried flowers on Mondays, promo on Tuesdays, farm life on Wednesdays, throwback on Thursdays, promo on Fridays", or can simply include a list of potential sources for content for days when you're really stuck.

The off season is also a great time to share the experiences you were too busy to share during the growing season. What were your biggest learning curves this year? What are you looking forward to next year? You still have a LOT to share with your audience, even if you're not selling fresh blooms until spring!

Honestly, once I got into the swing of posting about my farm, writing posts year round became less of a daily chore and much more of a running conversation with my audience. It's like micro-blogging, or light journalling. I'm almost constantly thinking about my business, so sometimes a post will be about a new flower I'm excited about, seeds I've ordered or started, or a more abstract idea that's been weighing on my mind. The only rule I have for myself is to keep the posts centred around the flower business. I never share political opinions or reveal too much about my personal life. I'm grateful for my following, and many of them are lovely people, but there's always a handful who are eager to argue or judge, and I'm just not interested in those interactions.

Riding the Emotional Waves of Online Engagement

There's an old Jerry Reed song titled, "When You're Hot, You're Hot", that has become my personal mantra when dealing with the highs and lows of online engagement. In the song, Reed jubilantly sings, "When you're hot you're hot! When you're not you're not! Put all the money in and let's roll em again! When you're hot you're hot!"

Somedays, a post will soar. Not only will it be seen, but it will spark something in your followers that will prompt them to engage. The notifications will roll in, a few sales will pop into your email inbox, and you'll feel like your business might not be the scariest thing in the world after all. A day later, you'll post an announcement for new services or a wonderful sale and... nothing. Nothing! Where did everyone go?? What went wrong? Did everyone simultaneously decide "nah, she actually kinda sucks"? Are they ignoring you? Why??

Let me be the first to tell you, you're fine. You did nothing wrong (unless the post was full of grammatical errors and disjointed ramblings, in which case, maybe you can do better!). Social media algorithms have become keenly attuned to our posting habits, as well as the emotions that run with them. Algorithms can recognize promotional-style posts via keywords like "new!" or "announcing!". They detect website urls (even ones that don't link), and phrases such as "click for more info". Sometimes, even simply saying "hey everyone!" could do it.

They don't want to give you free advertising, so when those bits of data are detected, they automatically stifle your post, limiting the number of followers who will see it in their feeds. This isn't a conspiracy, it's how the system actually works, and it will prompt you to panic, feel bad, then pay for a "boost". Preying on our insecurities is how these platforms make money, and it works!

The best way to circumvent this system, is by strategically wording your posts so they sound "personal", and by pacing out your promotions. I try to limit posts with detailed promotional content to about once per week. Then, in other posts, I casually refer back to "my last post" or "as I mentioned earlier this week"... which causes followers to peek back at the posts they may have missed due to algorithmic limitations. However, I don't do this robotically. My promotional posts aren't "Mondays only" or set to any routine, because I don't want my followers to tune me out. For the most part, I try to keep my posts as organic as possible.

I pay for sponsored content when I have something I want people outside my following to see, but I try to limit paid, sponsored, or "boosted" posts to no more than once a month. We discuss sponsored posts more under Purchased Advertising on p.143. The biggest benefit of sponsored posts is, if you spend a bit of extra time defining your target audience, they're a great way to pull in new local followers and potential customers. My follower count usually jumps about about 50 new follows per paid promotion, sometimes more.

Above: This photo of our sweet peas is one of our best performers online. Eventually, you'll get a sense of what content resonates the most effectively with your audience.

Just remember to pace out your content. Keep it real. Tell stories often, even if they're just daily nothings. Give give give, and only "ask" when you need to. Then refer back to those asks in a way that won't flag subsequent posts as "promotional content". It feels great to be "hot", but when you're not, don't panic. Just ride it out and work around it.

Most importantly, NEVER blame your followers. NEVER put the onus on them. I assume all of my followers are passive scrollers who just want to experience my farm in brief, lovely snippets. I don't ask them a lot of questions, they're busy! And I never resent them if my posts don't perform well. If they engage, I want it to be because they were genuinely inspired to do so. The quickest way to get muted, ignored, or unfollowed is by griping about low engagement online. Learn the game and be a better player.

Contests & Giveaways

Contests and giveaways are some of the most effective ways to reel in new followers and expand your online reach. The trick to making them work for you, is to have a very clear plan beforehand.

First off, define your goals. Are you trying to boost sales? Increase newsletter subscribers? Gain followers? Attract web traffic?

Next, decide what, exactly, you can afford to "give away". Don't overpromise. Offering a free bouquet seems easy enough to fulfill later on, but is that a custom bouquet, or a mixed market bouquet? Will that one "free" bouquet end up eating more time than you can afford during peak season?

Likewise, a bouquet subscription would be a GREAT prize to pull new people in, but be sure to think through the cost of labour, delivery, and all the other logistics that one subscription could potentially cost you.

For those reasons, it's very important to write out some clear terms and conditions regarding the product you plan to give away. Make those terms explicit when creating your post.

Now, decide how you want people to participate:

- "Tag us in your photo to enter!"
- "Include this post in your stories to enter!"
- "Caption this photo to win!"
- "Follow, like, share, or comment to enter!"
- "Vote here to enter!"

Next, decide on the length of your contest, and when you will choose/announce the winner. Make sure you include this information in your post!

Some social media platforms will actually shut down contests that go against their rules. Be sure to search "[platform] contest rules" online before running your contest.

Now you must decide whether you want to create a small promotional budget to further expand your reach outside of your current following. Most online platforms make it VERY easy to boost or promote a post.

Finally, decide on the image that will accompany your contest. This is a key part of running a successful campaign. Dig through your photo library and find the best images of your gardens, flowers, bouquets, and make sure the image is relevant to your contest. You want it to stop scrollers in their tracks!

I also avoid using images with text in them. Unless I have a beautiful photo with lots of empty space just perfect for text, I'd rather the photo speak for itself. I don't want my farm accounts to look like "business" accounts, because maintaining warmth and personality with my following is important to me, as it keeps the lines of conversation open.

If you don't have any stunning photos of your flowers yet, choose a simple image with a lot of open space, and then add text to it (there are many apps that can overlay text onto images). Make sure the image and the text

Right: Contests are a great way to pull eyes towards your business. Just remember that a lot of people might follow for the contest, and then unfollow if they don't win.

don't compete with each other, and above all, make it legible. Include the words "contest!" or "giveaway!" and then a quick description of the product you're giving away. Then, write all the other details of the contest clearly in the image caption below.

And once you have a winner, be sure to announce and congratulate them online! People love seeing "who won", and it brings formal closure to the contest.

Newsletters

Along with the many advantages your flowers have over other products, they also make the behind-the-scenes aspects of your business fun and easy to share. The life of growing flowers is interesting not only to your customers, but to other growers as well. We all want to see what everyone else is up to, and if you have an easy system for sharing news, it becomes VERY easy to reach folks!

While there are systems like Mailchimp to send out newsletters, my favourite so far is Wix's "Email Marketing" function. Through it, I can create newsletters that go out to everyone who has subscribed to my website. I have a simple "newsletter sign up" form on every page of my website, and it's been very effective in building my distribution lists. In my first season (from January to October), Alberta Girl Acres gained 324 newsletter subscribers. All were folks who popped onto my website, liked what they saw, and wanted to know more. I didn't have to push, hassle, or hype. As of 2020 (three years later), I have a subscriber base of around 750 people. When I want to reach the people who actually care about my business, I know a newsletter is the most direct route. Easy peasy!

From my website editing page, I can go straight to all my previous newsletters, reuse a template, and fill it with all my latest farm news. People can respond directly to the newsletter to reach me, or I can redirect people to various links on my website. It's

What a year. So much tha... SENT

Sent on: December 20, 2019 at 1:15 PM

294 **6**

OPENED CLICKED

Reuse

Above: I use a newsletter to communicate important info to my audience.

wonderful.

Once again, according to Canada's Anti-Spam Legislation, it is illegal to add any person's email address to a distribution list without their consent. All subscribers have to have signed up willingly. Not only is adding people to your lists without their knowledge illegal, it will also REALLY annoy them. Think about all the spam you get in a day. It doesn't matter if it's a sweet little flower farm, if they added you to their list without your permission, it's going to annoy you. It's just bad business (and is usually illegal).

Traditional Media
(Radio, TV, Print)

First and foremost, we live in a climate of VERY MESSY traditional media. Over the past decade in Canada, print media has been all but gutted of journalists, with funding cuts and massive layoffs resulting in special interest groups taking over and consolidating the few remaining outlets. (Google "Sun Media layoffs" and "Postmedia layoffs" for more context). There are VERY FEW full-time journalists left reporting in Canadian cities, and many are stretched extremely thin as they try to cover news that entire teams previously covered. For this reason, "media releases", ie: formal documents or emails announcing news about your business, are no longer effective tools for reaching media.

In your early years, the best way to "be seen" by the media, and to a greater extent, the public, is to piggy back and get involved with other exciting local initiatives. Farmer's markets, festivals, county fairs... these larger community projects and events often have their own marketing committees and strategies, and if you have a strong brand presence and clear messaging in place, paired with engaged social media followers who might spread the word, getting involved can easily result in getting a bit of fun coverage for your business. This is a very good first step, and from here, your foot is in the door re:

pulling in public interest.

Once again, this is where having a good website is KEY. Every out-of-the-blue media request I received in my first year — Alberta Views, The Western Producer, CBC Eyeopener, Sun Country Radio, Atlas Obscura, PBS — came through my website contact form. Make it as easy as possible for people to find you. This means having professional social media accounts, a clear website, and optimizing your website's SEO (Search Engine Optimization), so your business shows up when people google you.

During your early years, receiving attention from reputable media sources can feel like winning the lottery. Maybe an editor stumbled across your Instagram feed, or a CSA member has sweet connections. Suddenly, an entire town, city, or community is curious about your business, and inquiries start pouring in! It's time to put on your best PR boots and show the world your sweet sweet business!

If you find yourself in the middle of "media buzz", the first thing you should do is review your communications and PR policies and strategies. Prepare yourself and keep your head clear. If you have a team, notify them about what's happening, since it may affect them as well (ie: followers may filter over to your employees accounts to get a more fulsome look at the farming experience), and remind them of your key messaging and PR policies.

From there, ride the wave as professionally as you can! Media attention can quickly become overwhelming, so just hold the course and keep showing off your pretty product!

If you're ready for it, all that attention can obviously work very well for your business. This is where you'll be extremely thankful for your clear website with streamlined processes for incoming inquiries. You want all those inquiries filtered neatly into your inbox, so the administrative labour that goes into answering them is used as efficiently as possible.

It's also important to note that there is such thing as overexposure when it comes to media attention, especially for new businesses. If you're not ready for waves of public interest, it can quickly become a frustrating disaster. Losing track of orders, mixed up messaging, lost opportunities... your early years should be about starting slow and building your business in a sustainable way, so don't worry if you don't get a fun feature in your first season! Focus on building the best possible business you can, and then when the attention comes, you'll be more than ready for it.

This also means learning how and when to say no. Media attention can be extremely tempting, but like we talked about in our Public Relations section (p.65), sometimes the media has their own agenda or story in mind, and it might not actually benefit your business. Sometimes it hurts to say no, but steering your business in the right direction comes first.

Signage & Display

This is where your logo and branding come into heavy play. In your early years, the best advice I can offer is this:

If you have a farm stand, farmer's market table, flower truck, or any other space you sell your blooms from, design it specifically for Instagram photos. Even if everything around you is pavement or junk piles, create a space where, when you look through that little square Instagram lens, your stand pops out as the most adorable little spot ever.
Stage it.

Within that little square lens, you should see your logo, signage with large, legible font (including your products, prices, social media handle and website), your brand's colour palette worked throughout, and multi-tired shelving or racks that present your product clearly, at the forefront, utilizing height and negative space. If this means building an innovative little facade (ie: a false "shop front", stage frame, or ranch-style gate) that you can easily set up in front of or behind your table, do it!

Create a space that is 100% "Insta ready", and people WILL share your sweet set up on social media, expanding your reach and boosting your marketing efforts. A photo of your business, shared and tagged by a stranger on social media, is as valuable as a sale.

For me, a modified horse trailer was the perfect solution to all those requirements. Its small size, mobility, built-in storage, ease of set up and tear down, and unique presentation consistently delighted people, and performed extremely well on social media.

If you're not familiar with designing signage, do some heavy googling and pinterest searches, and find set ups that pop. Then deconstruct them, noting why they work. Do they use black "chalkboard" style signage? What fonts are they using? How large is their logo? What kind of messaging do they have on their signage? What's their colour scheme? How have they set up their display stands? What do they use for shade? Is there a "theme"? Make a list of everything that pops, and then figure out how you can create similar elements, using your own style, branding, and vision.

Word of Mouth

This falls right back into making your business as CUTE, BEAUTIFUL, DAZZLING, EYE CATCHING, CHARMING, DREAMY — or whatever other fun adjective suits your business — as possible! You want to leave an impression, so that when people see your product, the first thing they to do is tell their friends about it!

Dreamy workshops, cute market stands, gorgeous CSA bouquets (wrapped in paper with your logo!), and occasional advertisements saying "hey! We're here!", are all great ways to get people talking about your sweet little business.

Word of mouth takes a little more time to establish, but all the hard work you put into growing gorgeous blooms and taking care of those around you WILL eventually pay off (which shouldn't be your motivation, obviously! But it's a nice plus!). Be patient, hold the course, and do good work. People will notice and appreciate it, and the rewards will come.

Purchased Advertising

When launching important news, such as your new business, new products, CSAs, or workshops, it sometimes helps to set aside a small budget for purchased advertising. In your first year, this budget doesn't have to be extravagant, but a little can go a long way if you time the launch just right, and target the right demographics.

First off, WHERE should you advertise?

Traditional media is one option, however print often requires a long lead time, and is quite expensive given the number of people you're likely to reach. Considering how fresh you are to your business, you also don't want to lock yourself into costly advertising that might actually require more flexibility due to your growing season's ups and downs.

Likewise, many local lifestyle magazines and newspaper sections offer "sponsored content" options, where you essentially write an article yourself and pay to have it run. Fees for this kind of advertising are usually a couple thousand dollars, so again, consider whether it will suit your budget, and the fluctuating nature of your new business.

The best form of paid advertising for small business is through social media "boosted" posts, sponsored content, and paid ads. As problematic as social media is, its primary design is to sell content, and when you step over to the advertiser's side of it, it's actually incredibly useful.

Once you have a business page on Facebook, and a business account on Instagram, the platforms go to a lot of effort to train you in how to boost and promote your content. It's actually very annoying, BUT, for newbies, still quite helpful. Businesses have control over their content, budget, length of promotion, and targeted demographics, and if your featured image is clean, eye-catching, and includes clear messaging, you'll stand out in other user's feeds.

Tourism Listings

If you have a few successful workshops under your belt, or if your farm is set up for public visits, you might be ready to step into the wonderful world of local tourism.

Whether you advertise through your local tourism websites, or sign up as a host for Airbnb "experiences", positioning your business within the realm of tourism could lead to wonderful new opportunities and revenue streams. Just be sure to have a firm sense of WHAT you're offering, and make sure all of your booking and transaction processes are air tight.

Additionally, on platforms such as Airbnb, you don't have to make your exact location known until guests have confirmed their booking, which is a big plus in terms of security and privacy.

Right: Another Airbnb host in our area made us aware of Airbnb "experiences", which are a perfect fit for our business!

Flower Farm Floral Arrangement Workshop

📍 VULCAN

🕐 2.5 hours total

▤ Drinks and Equipment

💬 Offered in English

Photography

Left page: An arrangement created by one of our summer workshop guests. I take photos of all our guests' creations, and then send them to guests following the workshops.

Photography;

Finding Your Angle

Following a flower farm on social media offers an endless stream of pristine photos, but if you were to actually visit one of those farms, you may be surprised by how different they look in person. Farms that appear as pastoral, sun streaked dreams in our feeds don't usually look quite so heavenly in real life. In my first year, I had several people ask to come visit my farm, and when they arrived I could see the confusion on their faces; "so, uhmm, is this it??". Yep that was it! My farm was abandoned for 30 years before I bought it. Our first year was a mess. The photos I was posting were angled very carefully to show only the prettiest nooks and cutest crannies. The rest of it was a categorical shite box.

A flower farm is still a farm; old scrap piles, half completed projects in every corner, machines waiting to be fixed, fandangled inventions that didn't quite work out, busted fences, minefields of animal poop, abandoned equipment, livestock jailbreaks, relentless weed invasions… farms are microcosms of barely controlled chaos.

For those who take pride in their properties, a fledgling farm will eventually morph into the gorgeous, dappled scenes we all work so hard to emanate, but even then, there will always be utilitarian photobombs lurking around every corner.

Above: These two photos were taken of the same field, on the same day, and at the same time of day. The first photo is okay, but doesn't showcase the garden very well. The second photo was taken facing the sun, but cropping it out so that only a few rays came through in the photo, creating a much dreamier effect. I also crouched behind the laceflower, so the viewer has a clear sense of foreground, middleground, and background. We also see the prairie horizon in the distance. The second photo works much more effectively at telling the story of our prairie farm, while also showing off our blooms.

This is where finding your angle becomes extremely important in terms of marketing.

Two of the most beautiful Instagram accounts I follow are Charlie McCormick (mccormickcharlie) and Janet Tuenschel (countrycutflowers). They have both utilized very specific, very picturesque angles of their farms, to stunning effect. Charlie with his gorgeous, rolling informal gardens in the Scottish countryside, backed by old world cottages of stone, and Janet, with her lovely rows of tended blooms, poised in front of a grand red barn and the misty rolling vistas of Southern Ontario.

A specific view of your farm can define a large part of your online brand. It brings your followers "back home", pinging their brains as they scroll through their feeds, reminding them of a lovely, familiar dream.

PHOTO TIPS

Composition

Get low. Think in terms of "feature", "foreground", and "background". We want to see the feature element clearly, but showing some of the landscape behind your gardens goes a long way in terms of setting a scene and telling your story.

Keep the horizon level. If we can see the horizon, it should be straight across, not tilted. A level horizon brings a sense of professionalism and harmony to your photos. If you have a hilly background, just try to imagine where the straight horizon would be, and keep the photo as level as possible.

Consider the "weight" of your composition. Is there a lot happening on one side of the photo, and not much on the other? Try to keep the elements balanced.

Fill the frame but try not to crop the feature element. For armload shots: As you position the feature element in your photo, pay attention to each edge of the frame. Get the bunch or bouquet as close as you can to the edges, without cropping it.

Take tons of "full frame" shots. Whether you have twenty buckets full of CSA bouquets, or a gorgeous, full harvest set out in your workshop, snap some "full frame" shots and save them for future use. A full frame shot is exactly what it sounds like: the entire frame crammed with nothing but flowers. These photos will come in extremely handy for marketing, and can be used as backgrounds, banners, or transferred to merchandise.

Take plenty of "empty space" photos too. A photo that's mostly sky, or with featured elements arranged in a lower corner with plenty of open space above, or a rustic, plain surface with a few flowers placed at the edges, these are all photos you can easily add text to later. Perfect for announcements, invites, and advertisements.

Focus

Hold your stem, bunch or bouquet outwards, towards the camera. We want to see those blooms! The look of detailed, in-focus blooms with an out-of-focus background is especially effective.

Adjust the focus on the feature element. This goes for armload shots and garden shots. With smart phones, you can tap and hold to focus in on a specific element in the photo. With cameras, you can use auto or manual focus settings to make the feature element as clear as possible. Clear focus is everything. If nothing else, we need to be able to see your flowers clearly.

You don't want the sun to be directly behind your subjects, but off in the corner creates a lovely effect.

Lighting

Nothing makes your photos look dreamier than the light of early morning or early evening. Keep the sun tucked into the corners of your compositions, allowing the lens to capture streaks of sunlight. Backlit compositions tend to offer more aesthetic value, however if you need your audience to see true colours, side-lighting or lightly shaded shots may be necessary to get a better view of your blooms.

Overcast days are ideal for daytime photos. If in bright daylight, find a shady spot under a tree. Bright sunlight creates extreme contrasts in your photos that make it hard to see flowers, faces, and garden details. Even better, position the flowers in the shade and fill the background with a bright, sunny landscape.

Use outbuilding interiors for photo shoots. Try setting up a small shoot inside a rustic outbuilding like a barn, shed, or quonset. Leave the large door open, and position your shoot inside the building, just beyond where the sunlight reaches. You don't want direct sunlight, but the light from the open door paired with the darkness of the inside of the building will create an elegant contrast in your photos. Bump it up another level by hanging a black or white sheet behind your flowers.

Above: this photo is untouched, and was taken inside our quonset using natural light and a makeshift tripod. My camera has a "remote live view shooting" feature that allows me to connect it to my phone via wifi. I was actually holding my phone in my left hand, seeing what the camera was seeing, and adjusting the composition accordingly. I could adjust the camera's focus with my phone, and with a simple tap, could shoot as many remote photos as I needed.

Setting the Stage

In my first year, I was fortuitously contacted by an elementary school that was seeking a home for their old theatre curtains. Though I didn't have a clear plan for them at the time, I jumped at the offer, knowing I would find a purpose for them eventually. Now, they hang in our workshop space, and make for a simple, elegant backdrop for all of our workshops.

A textile artist also gifted me with a black, single panel curtain made from a velvety material that absorbs light beautifully. If I don't want to use the blue of the theatre curtains as a background for arrangements and bouquets, I can simply pin the black curtain up instead.

Those materials, paired with the natural light afforded by the large quonset door (essentially a massive garage door) and the building's dark interior, have created a simple, almost effortless area for photoshoots. Our photos look professional quality, without the professional expense.

Left: A bumblebee tackles the larkspur. This was taken using my basic Canon EOS Rebel T6.

Cameras

Invest in a good camera. Your flowers are your key marketing asset. Their beauty, and everything they represent, are your crown jewels. You *must* to be able to capture them effectively and consistently. You don't need a super expensive, professional-grade camera, but having a smartphone with a good quality, built-in camera, or even a basic hand held digital camera for impromptu shoots, will pay off again and again as you get your business off the ground.

And yes, there will be photographers who will want to visit (charge them!), and there will be many opportunities to trade photos for flowers, but having the ability to capture your pretties in-the-moment, and share your gardens from your own perspective, is absolutely imperative if you want to engage followers and customers in an honest way. Remember, there are two types of feeds that you don't want to get lost in: the slick, soulless, "perfect" blogger style that currently saturates social media, and the awkward, poorly lit, ill-considered style of someone new to the internet. Somewhere in the middle, you need to find your place. Your feed doesn't have to look professional, but it should look considered. Intentional. Loved.

Me holding my Canon EOS Rebel T6. It's been an essential tool for documenting my blooms and marketing my farm.

In my first year, I had an old iphone SE. It took decent photos when the light was bright enough, but otherwise my photos looked... amateur. Grainy, not enough detail, the resolution never looked right. My farmhand happened to have a beautiful camera and a keen eye, and was willing to capture shots when time allowed. Hoever, even though she was on the farm most days, the added step of me seeing something, thinking "oh yes that's nice", and then interrupting her work to ask her to snap a photo, then trying to explain what I was seeing and what I wanted her to capture... it wasn't an ideal process. I wanted to share what my eyes were seeing, when I was seeing it. My phone fell short, I needed something better.

That Christmas, my wonderful boyfriend got me the perfect "starter camera", a Canon EOS Rebel T6 with an 18-55mm DC III lens. The camera is very easy to use, takes wonderful photos, and has a super handy wifi function that connects to my phone for remote shooting and easy transfers.

The whole package cost about $600 CAD. A very worthy investment, especially considering how much I've used it. I've still only just begun to explore its settings, and I have plenty of time to dive deeper into lenses and accessories without worrying about the camera going obsolete in a few years.

Left: A dried flower arrangement, enhanced using editing features such as "light" and "vignette".

Retouching and Filters

There will be occasional pristine moments, when no touch ups or filters will be necessary. But even the most skilled photographers retouch their photos. Instagram offers plenty of retouching options, from manual adjustments to filters, but basic photo editing software like Adobe Lightroom, or even your phone's photo editing settings are super handy, and well worth familiarizing yourself with.

Everyone has their own preferences. I avoid filters, because they just look too... filtered. They often change the unique lighting that our big Alberta skies naturally offer, homogenizing my shots into the ever flowing feed of "Insta pics". I don't want my farm to look like every other instagram farm. I want it to look like MY farm. The photo editing settings I use most often are "exposure", "brightness", "contrast", and "tilt". I rarely adjust the photo more than 10 points from its original version.

You don't have to be a professional photographer to show off your gorgeous flowers. With a decent camera and some attention paid to lighting and composition, your accounts will be bursting with gorgeous images of your farm.

Every Photo Tells a Story

Whether you're snapping a photo of one superstar bloom, an especially healthy patch of the garden, or a full day's harvest, every photo has the potential to tell a little bit more of your story. Your story is what inspires your followers. It's what keeps them engaged and empathetic to your adventure. This is why it's so important to consider your background in every photo. For example, a barn is a clear visual cue that you are, indeed, a farm. Farms have history, they speak to hard, "honest" work, and to generations of families tending the soil. Many who weren't raised on farms have pastoral, romanticized ideas of what farm life is like. Feed those fantasies!

Likewise, if you have constant cloudy days, or dry, relentless sunshine, show us! We want to know what you're contending with. If you have a bouquet making workspace, give us a glimpse! If you have chickens, let's see them scritching around in the background. Do your pets follow you around during the day? Is there a feral barn cat that occasionally pops its head out? We would love to see their furry faces among your gorgeous gardens. So many who follow you are living vicariously through your feed. Fill it with all the little pieces of your "dreamy" life, while keeping your flowers front and centre.

Above all: TAKE A LOT OF PHOTOS. Do you have a field full of blooms with nowhere to go? As disappointing as that may feel in the moment, it's actually very rare that we get to see our flowers in full bloom, since we're cutting them so often! Take a million photos

Above: A diva dahlia.

and save them for later. Enjoy them. Use them. You may decide you want to promote a new service in the winter that needs a pretty photo to go along with it, or a magazine may contact you in the off season wanting to do a feature. When none of your flowers are in full bloom, you'll still want to show them off! Take photos when you can!!

I use photos as seasonal notes too. Because most photo album apps save images according to date, I can easily scroll through the previous year to see what was blooming when. This is a quick and easy way to keep track of successes and failures, to plan future beds.

Hauling our flower trailer to the market.

Operations & Management

A big part of your work as a business owner will be identifying and developing operational routines and processes, and leading during times of stress and uncertainty. As we discussed back in our RISK section, there will be plenty of ups and downs as you step into this adventure. It's your job to hold the course and lead with a steady hand.

Distribution

"Distribution" is the process of getting your blooms into the hands of your eager customers. Without a doubt, the biggest and most difficult learning curve when we started was figuring out how to move (LITERALLY move) all our blooms in our first year.

When you're first starting out, it's unlikely that you'll be producing enough reliable blooms to work with a distributor, or similar intermediary. For the time being, distribution is more or less wholly on you. This is an easily overlooked piece of the puzzle. How hard can moving a few flowers be, right? Okay, well, let's see…

First, how many blooms are we talking?

In our first year, we grew enough for 50 to 70 bouquets per week, plus about 30 bunches. We fit approx four bouquets or bunches in each black pail, which meant we had around 25 to 30 pails per week. So, 25 to 30 pails of flowers, with water and supplies, went to the market each Saturday.

Whether or not you're working a farmers market, you'll need a vehicle. Depending on how many flowers you plan to grow and sell, you'll need an *air conditioned* vehicle with good cargo capacity. Blooms will NOT transport well in the summer heat without air conditioning. And despite all the gorgeous photos you've seen of flowers in the back of a pick up truck, you can't just pop your blooms into an open truck bed, unless your destination is less than 100 feet away and you plan on driving very, very slowly.

Doing deliveries? You'll want something fuel efficient. What is your fuel budget?

Hiring someone else to do deliveries? THEY'LL need something fuel efficient, with cargo capacity. Does this mean you'll need two vehicles? One to take blooms to your delivery person, and one for your delivery person to drive?

Do you plan on transporting blooms every day? Once a week? Are you planning on having pick-up points for your CSA members? Where will those be? Who will deliver your flowers to those locations?

If you plan to install wedding flowers, you'll need something that can manage anywhere from a few bouquets to larger installations (depending on the services you offer, of course). If you plan to work solely with florists, a wagon-style vehicle would likely be enough. For big farm-to-city hauls, larger cargo vans or cube vans might be better options.

Planning on a modified trailer? You'll need a vehicle that can haul it. A truck doesn't have much cargo capacity though. Will your trailer have cargo capacity? Will it be insulated? Air conditioned?

And lastly, do you have a family? Will your delivery errands merge with your parenting errands? Does your cargo vehicle need to have passenger capacity as well?

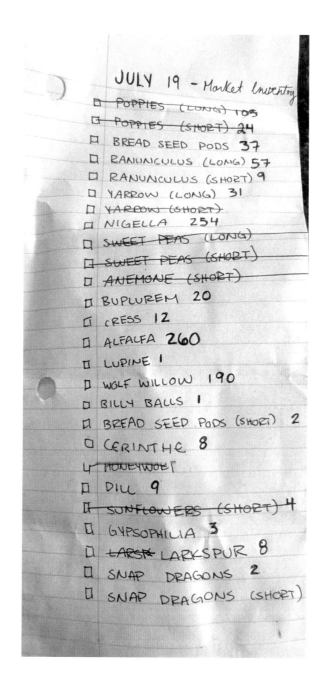

My kids were great sports as we figured out our farm's daily routines, but as you can see from my daughter's face, flower deliveries weren't their favourite!

Again, it all depends on your scale and your market, but the logistics of distribution can get REALLY tricky if you plan on serving multiple markets. The style and capacity of the vehicle you choose will all depend on which market(s) you choose to serve.

Throughout our entire first season, our easy peasy plans were often screeched to a halt by transport logistics. We juggled between two different vehicles; our Prius V for 16 pails or less, our Pathfinder plus flower trailer for 16+ pails, and both vehicles plus the trailer for especially large loads. And of course, if the kids were coming with us, that shifted everything. Since that time, I've worked hard to bring our market to us, rather than distribute to them. Our focus has changed to on-farm sales and workshops, a farmer's market closer to our farm, and fewer CSA subscriptions.

Distribution and transportation is definitely a puzzle at first, but once you settle into your markets, the logistics will settle too.

YOUR OFFICE

If you're entrepreneurially inclined, chances are you already have a nook carved out where you can work and dream, or maybe your family has an office for finances and computer tasks. While establishing your business, it's very important that you have a space JUST for you and all the administration that your venture will require.

Everyone works differently, and some methods of organization that I swear by might make zero sense to someone else. However, I do think it's crucial that you equip your office space with the following elements:

1. A Computer.

Whether laptop or desktop, you'll need something that can handle online work, bookkeeping software, and if you have the skills, graphic and web design. In terms of software, I recommend having Microsoft Office or equivalent, Adobe Acrobat, and a decent photo editing program (ie: Adobe Photoshop or Lightroom). In terms of digital filing and content management, I use my own processes (labelled, dated folders and subfolders) and G-Suite.

2. A Desk (and chair, obviously).

Many of us have reliably used the kitchen table for years as hobby gardeners, but trust me, you'll need a desk and a comfortable chair for your business. Your space will quickly pile up with invoices, notebooks, reading material, seeds, and so on, and you really don't want anyone else messing with your controlled chaos.

3. A Filing Cabinet.

It doesn't have to be big, but you'll need at least two drawers to file away all your paperwork such as invoices, receipts, insurance policies, bills of sale, and so on. It's possible to do a lot of business digitally now, but it's still essential to keep paper copies of your business dealings and transactions.

4. An Accessible Storage System for Seeds.

While I keep detailed lists of my seed inventory on my computer, I've found it's still necessary to have all my seeds on hand as I edit the website, answer queries, or update my planting plans. I use a tupperware drawer tower, and have organized my seeds as annuals and perennials, alphabetically. Some seeds require stratification in the fridge or freezer however, so check the packet instructions re: how to best store them.

5. A Printer.

Depending on your needs, you may use your printer frequently (coupons, workshop materials, invoices), or rarely. Because they're so cheap to buy, you should also get a printer with scanning and photocopying capabilities.

6. A Bookshelf.

Even a small one will do, but all those gorgeous books on growing beautiful blooms and running a business need a home, and you'll want them within arms reach while planning and strategizing year after year.

7. Lighting.

You'll need to be able to see while you work, and you'll frequently find yourself plugging away at your desk long after the sun has set. Lighting can transform an otherwise drab space into something warm and appealing.

8. Office Supplies Storage.

Reams of paper, mailing envelopes of all sizes, scotch tape, post-it notes, staplers, pens, notebooks, file folders, stamps... all these things get used frequently, and should be a few convenient steps from your desk.

Your office should be a place where you feel GOOD doing work. Take the time to set up a space just for you, with a tidy system for filing and organizing. You'll thank yourself!

Below: my office has since outgrown this living room nook, and now takes up half of my bedroom. It won't be long before I'll have to expand again. Businesses take space!

OPERATIONAL TIPS

Starting out, many of your operational processes will be very basic, and as your business evolves, you'll find more involved management systems that work best for you. Here are a few operational newbie tips:

Separate all your accounts (social media, credit card, banking, etc) from your personal accounts.

Have a tight filing system, both for hard and digital copies. Look up "file organization tips" online if you're new to filing.

Learn spreadsheet software and make spreadsheets your friend! For seed inventories, wish lists, resources, memberships, etc, spreadsheets truly make life easier once you've pushed through learning how to use them. I use Google Sheets, and it works great for me.

Use bookkeeping software that allows for online invoicing and payments. I use Paypal for this, and it works wonderfully. If Paypal isn't your thing, ask your personal network for suggestions! Quickbooks offers online invoicing and payments (for additional fees), and many website platforms do as well (ie: my Wix site does, however I prefer Paypal).

Keep a visible calendar or two near your desk or on your desktop. I have a four month dry-erase calendar on my wall beside me as I work, and it changes often. I also keep an online business calendar (via Google) to share with my farm helpers, and to set reminders.

SAVE ALL YOUR RECEIPTS. If it means jamming them into a large envelop to sort later, or filing them month by month, always save them. Plus hard copy bank statements, invoices, payroll records (if applicable), and any other material that supports an item of income, deduction, or credit shown on your tax return.

Pay people on time. If it means you have to set reminders or schedule the payments as automatic transfers, do it! Nothing is worse than owing money to people who worked hard for you (and were promised pay).

Write job descriptions for hired help and volunteers. Doing so will clarify expectations, both for you and those helping you. Google similar job descriptions and use them as templates. If, over time, you have to edit the descriptions or add responsibilities to anyone's workload, be sure to have a conversation with your help about the changes first.

Set aside a few weeks during the slow season as your "benchmark analysis" period. Take some time to grind through all the receipt sorting, new year strategizing, business plan rewrites, and amended projections. The ideal time for this would right before tax time (ugh).

Speaking of "ugh", unless you're well versed in small farm accounting, *hire an accountant to do your taxes*. Maybe someone willing to trade their services for a free CSA...

Our flower trailer, mid-facelift.

Monthly & Daily Operations

It's very likely that your early experiences will look completely different than mine, and your day-to-day routines and challenges will depend on your market streams and how high a bar you set for yourself from the beginning. Every day creates new challenges, and after a few years of farming, our running joke is still "every problem is 20 problems in disguise".

In the following pages, I've included a general look at our first year of monthly operations. It was a ridiculously busy spring, but I didn't actually live on my farm until April of our first spring, which was why we dug beds in the spring, rather than the fall. Ideally, you'll want to prep all your beds in the fall, then amend them in the spring.

Also, if there had already been more established perennials on the farm, we wouldn't have been in such a tough spot when spring came and we had to start fulfilling CSAs while also stocking our trailer for the market. We have a 25' X 100' unheated greenhouse now, which extends our season nicely, ensuring we have blooms in June after the tulips and daffodils have stopped producing.

A misty view of our "workshop garden". We built our greenhouse close enough to both quonsets to make harvests and workshop tours more efficient.

YEAR ONE MONTHLY SCHEDULE

January
- Launched website
- Began gathering newsletter subscribers
- Planned flower beds
- Purchased seeds
- Read and researched
- Began Floret 6 week course
- Startup loan disbursement and payments commenced

February
- Planned flower beds
- Purchased seeds
- Read and researched
- Sent out first newsletter
- Began starting seeds (many started way too early)
- Began advertising and selling CSAs
- Completed Floret 6 week course
- Applied for and received youth employment grant

March
- Planned beds
- Purchased seeds (impulse purchases at this point)
- Started seeds indoors
- Advertised and sold CSAs
- Committed to farmer's market (which ran on Saturdays, June to October)

April
- SNOW
- MORE SNOW?! (third week of April)
- Frantically began breaking ground wherever was thawed enough
- Started seeds indoors
- Made backup plan for CSAs, which were due to start in May
- Finished assembling the greenhouse frame, no plastic yet

May
- Ground thawed by mid-May
- We continued frantically prepping beds
- Planted maybe half the seeds I had purchased
- Planted seedlings after last frost (usually the thrid week of May for us)
- Made adjustments to our CSA subscriptions, while apologizing to our subscribers
- Installed drip irrigation
- Modified horse trailer/flower trailer
- Harvested our first sparse tulips
- Hosted 3 wwoofers for 3 weeks
- Built other infrastructure
- Mowed and planted small cherry tree orchard

June
- NO FLOWERS (I actually got anxiety remembering this)
- Frantic daily foraging to fulfill CSAs and market bouuqets
- Attended our weekly Saturday farmer's market (1.5 hours away)
- Built walk-in cooler
- WEEDING
- Plans to succession plant did not happen, too much going on
- Built workshop space
- Hosted our first floral arrangement workshop
- Media buzz over my "plant rescue" service, which got out of hand. Too much driving and labour for no return.
- Planted 150 trees and shrubs on the farm (less than half survived, but they were cheap baby "sticks", so it wasn't a huge loss, aside from labour)
- Put landscape fabric down over alfalfa field to prep it for flowers the following year.

*Our very first farm grown tulips.
These went straight to my mom!*

YEAR ONE MONTHLY SCHEDULE

July
- No farm flowers until mid-July
- Frantic foraging continued for the first two weeks of July
- Attended our weekly Saturday farmer's market (1.5 hours away)
- Delivered weekly CSAs
- Created a flower processing and bouquet making space in our outbuilding
- Hosted workshops on the farm
- WEEDING
- Early morning (6am) harvests began mid month
- Spent afternoons creating market bouquets
- Target financial projections were not being met, sought additional credit to cover cash flow gaps
- Began pressing and drying flowers
- Regular pest spraying began (we should have been mitigating pests since April though)

August
- So many flowers! Bliss!
- Attended our weekly Saturday farmer's market (1.5 hours away)
- Delivered weekly CSAs
- Hosted workshops on the farm
- Continued early morning harvests & afternoon bouquet making
- Began advertising our "Surviving Year One" business course
- Briefly sold through the local grocery store

September
- EARLY FROST, FLOWERS DONE. CUE MILD PANIC
- Cancelled our remaining farmer's market dates
- Ended farmhand's contract one month early
- Turned focus to dried flowers

September (cont'd)
- Advertised business course
- Final CSA flower deliveries (with the promise of holiday wreaths later)
- Final floral workshops
- Covered greenhouse with poly (better late than never)
- Dug and prepped flower beds for following year
- Ordered fall bulbs (should have ordered them in the spring)
- Planned next year's beds and ordered seeds

October
- Submitted grant report
- Planted fall bulbs
- Dug dahlias
- Prepped business course
- Began next year's CSAs waiting list
- Created & delivered CSA wreaths
- Prepped greenhouse for spring planting, moved chickens in.

November
- Continued creating and delivering CSA wreaths
- Hosted business course sessions
- Began winter "value-added" projects with pressed flowers

December
- Worked on "value-added" projects
- Recieved difficult family news, paused all business
- Requested portion of "back up" line of credit from funding group to cover cash flow gaps.
- Took personal downtime with family.

My daughter helping out. Family helpers should be given the same considerations as paid staff would be. Especially in terms of schedules and safety.

HUMAN RELATIONS (HR)

HR refers to training, hiring, and managing staff and team members; creating their work schedules, delegating workloads, ensuring work is completed competently and safely, keeping a harmonious balance among staff, and culling (firing) those who are unhealthy for your business.

In your first year, it may be that you're the only human you need to worry about, or the only other people involved with your business are friends and family you already have established relationships with. But that doesn't negate the need for HR! If anything, it makes it a bit more complicated. It's hard to be The Boss when your mother is giving her valuable time to help you out, but it's still on you to train, delegate, and ensure the work gets done properly.

One well-meaning, but wayward team member can kill or set back an entire crop, costing you thousands of dollars in lost revenue. So how do you get around the awkwardness of being The Boss when you're also desperately grateful for any help you can get?

There's one tried and true strategy for being a "good boss"; it's called the Sandwich Method, and it's very simple:

It starts with bread, ie: praise, like "this looks great! I love how you [insert something great they did]".

Then you get to the meat, addressing what needs improvement in a non blameful way, like "one thing we might run into if we don't plant these deep enough, is the root balls will dry out…"

Then you add some veggies, ie: "would you mind planting these all a bit deeper?". Do a quick demo for them, so it's very clear.

Then more bread! "These are going to come up really nicely, thanks for helping out!".

And the words "WE" or "LET'S" are very helpful when training and guiding your team.

If someone drops a tray of seedlings, saying "no problem, let's salvage as much as we can!" sounds much better than "can you pick those up and save as many as you can?". It's a method of sharing the weight of responsibility by making them feel like you're right there with them.

This doesn't mean you have to physically do every task or fix every problem with them, but changing your language so they feel less personally responsible for slips and accidents (because there will be many!) will keep everyone feeling much lighter. People know when they've messed up, offer your support, and guide them up and out of getting stuck in a negative headspace.

In addition to raising your fledgling baby business, as the owner you'll have to do a lot of personal work to learn how to communicate under stress. Your support team is your life line, and your primary job is to treat them well. No snapping. No blaming. Remember to breathe. If they've signed up to join you on this ridiculous ride, it's because they believe in you and your vision, and that is a precious gift.

Learn healthy ways to vent. Learn how to teach, train and explore ideas without making anyone feel small. Do not indulge in industry gossip, drama, or beefs (especially online!). Learn how to empower and inspire, and your circle of support will not only stay with you, but continue

to grow.

Empower your team. I can't stress enough how important it is to trust and empower the people who help you on a day to day basis. Let them know you trust them. Thank them. Be gentle when stress is high.

Do what you can to diplomatically resolve personality conflicts. Especially in the case of working on a farm, many of your team won't really have anywhere to retreat to if they need to blow off steam. Keeping the peace is best for everyone's morale.

Make your business safe for all. There are many online resources that detail occupational health and safety for different regions and business types. Be sure to research the insurance and potential training your business will require in order to keep everyone who enters your property safe. For the most part, farms should have General Commercial Liability policies in place to protect owners and employees.

Be sure to carefully assess the skills of anyone who has come to work or help out on your farm. Never assume someone knows how to safely use a piece of equipment. And it's of course imperative that YOU competently understand the equipment before handing it over to anyone else. Even something as simple as a handheld post pounder can cause a major injury. Always train, do quick demos, and supervise as they learn. And never give toxic sprays or corrosive cleaners to volunteers or untrained staff. The risk of something going wrong, for both the users and your plants, is just too high.

Beyond physical safety, take emotional safety into account as well. Implementing formal "zero tolerance" policies and procedures regarding harassment and inappropriate behaviour can go a long way if you choose to host interns or hire multiple staff. This is especially applicable if you plan to bring on seasonal labour or WWOOFers (volunteers of the World Wide Opportunities on Organic Farms, www.wwoof.net). It will make dealing with those rare scenarios much easier.

As an employer, learn how to be an "active bystander", and how to identify when someone is being picked on or made to feel uncomfortable. Ensure that your policies include the ability to terminate staff upon submission of formal complaints, and make sure each employee is fully aware of those policies, so that if you're not witness to the behaviour but believe the victim, you still have a way of culling the offender without being liable for wrongful dismissal. Cut toxic people out of your ranks, and explain to them why, reminding them of your policy, so going forward they know their behaviour was unacceptable.

HR is one of the least "dreamy" elements to building your flowery business, but it falls into essential strategic planning and risk mitigation, and will better equip you when sticky times emerge down the road.

My boyfriend Nathan helping with the harvest.

Your Team & Allocating Labour

NO ONE CAN DO IT ALL

Early on, it's very important to identify what you CAN'T do. Online, you may see flower farmers who appear to be doing it all with ease. The fact is, the ones who make it look easy have help, or have simply chosen not to share their struggles.

And, there are some who frequently post about their struggles, often detailing how hard they work, how thinly they stretch themselves, how tired they constantly are. Yes, flower farming is really hard, but you don't have to prove yourself by becoming a martyr to the dream. There is no award for burnout. There is no race to the bottom of your own mental health.

While your business is, in many ways, an entity separate from yourself, it's also very much YOU. And you need to take care of you, or the business, and you, will collapse.

It's OKAY to say "not yet", or "maybe next year". Reigning yourself in and starting slow, giving yourself time to process and learn, is good business. And of course, surround yourself with as many good, capable, skilled, and supportive people as you can find.

In my first year, my biggest worry was burning out, and bringing everyone down with me in the process. Asking for help was so hard. There is so much pressure on you, as the owner of a new business, to be in control; to know what you're doing at all times. And to be honest, it really *is* all on you. There's simply no way to defer that responsibility. You birthed this baby, and you're in charge of its growth and development.

Even if your "team" consists of yourself and a partner or friend, it's still a team! As you'll learn throughout this book, there is a LOT to get done in your early years, whatever your scale or market. Having at least one more capable and reliable person on board will double your productivity, often by virtue of the fact that *they add two more hands*.

Before jumping into your first season, take some time to identify all the potential labour required, and break down who will take on that labour.

My mother, myself, and my uncle Al. My family and their skills were absolutely invaluable to my farm in our first year.

In my first year, this is what my breakdown of labour looked like at the planning stage:

Sarah (Owner)	My Mother	Family, Friends, wwoofers	Contract
Marketing & Communications	Accounting & financials	Seasonal labour	Equipment repair
Crop planning & care	Seasonal labour		Building repair
Tilling & bed prep	Deliveries		Infrastructure construction
Strategic planning	Event hall management		
Workshop hosting			
Deliveries			

173

Right page: My "fall clean up crew". While I never let these floofs roam the gardens during the growing season, when our season ends they make wonderful weeders, fertilizers, and cultivators!

Now, looking back, that breakdown was fairly vague, and not entirely accurate (which is fair, I had no idea what was ahead!). Here's what our labour breakdown actually looked like:

As you can see, "MORAL SUPPORT" played almost as big a role as actual, physical labour did. I needed supportive people around me to lean on as I navigated the ongoing, intense learning curves.

Sarah	Hired Labour	Volunteers	My Mother	Family & Friends
Marketing & Communications	"Skilled" labour	General labour	Accounting	General labour
Strategic planning	Emergency pinch hitter	Household help	Financial support	Market support
Crop planning	Infrastructure construction		Deliveries	Vehicle support
"Skilled" labour	Permaculture research		Child care	Mechanical support
HR	MORAL SUPPORT		MORAL SUPPORT	Deliveries
Deliveries				MORAL SUPPORT
Market labour				
Workspace design				
Financials				
Web design & maintenance				

Above: My dear farmhand Kendra, on her last day of our second season.

Your breakdown of labour will depend on your own skills and the skills of those around you. Identifying your capabilities and capacities, as well as those of your team, will set you up for a much smoother ride.

And unless you have a true desire to develop new skills in unfamiliar fields (ie: website creation, carpentry, accounting, mechanics), DO NOT burden yourself with those tasks. Find someone who can handle them competently, whether a friend or family member. If they are willing to donate their time and skills, take it! As your seasons unfold, you'll find ways to compensate them, and in may cases you may see opportunities to create paid positions for those skills in the years ahead.

Just remember to acknowledge and thank those who help you. Even if your team is just a rag tag group of happy helpers, remember to lead with patience and graciousness. Good help is hard to find, so when you find it, hang onto it!

To Hire or Not to Hire?

One of the most difficult choices going into my first year was whether or not to hire someone. Wages are expensive, and as a brand new business, they feel like a huge cut into your cash flow. With options such as volunteer labour from WWOOF and Workaway, plus help from family and friends, added to the fact that farming would be my full-time job, I mulled HARD over whether or not I needed paid labour.

Fortuitously, I was contacted by a friend who had been volunteering on an organic farm in New Zealand. I had worked with her previously and knew she was an extremely capable and passionate person. She was very interested in working on my farm, and I knew immediately how much my business would benefit from her skills and attitude. I applied for a Canadian government grant called the Agricultural Youth Green Jobs Initiative, received funds to supplement her wages, and hired her for a five month contract. She stayed at my farm 3 days a week during that time, and I provided a cute camper for her accommodations.

I also brought on three WWOOFers for three weeks in the spring, and while every volunteer labourer is different, I'll share what I learned from our experience:

When both my hired hand and my volunteer WWOOFers arrived, I had only been living at my farm for one month. Four weeks of that month had been snow, and when everyone arrived at the beginning of May, I had NO idea what I was doing. I had no clue what our routines would be, which tasks took priority, or what the season held for us. All I knew was that I needed help.

Our WWOOFers were lovely, but my accommodations barely met their needs. Their living space was crowded, water was in constant shortage, my refrigerator was malfunctioning, and the dogs hassled them regularly. Putting four people to work, 6 hours a day, 5 days a week, when the ground is barely workable and you have no idea what you're doing is... hard.

The key to making it all work without anyone imploding? My hired hand. She arrived guns a-blazing, ready to MAKE IT HAPPEN. I was able to delegate a lot of the farm's to-do lists to her, which she then assigned to our volunteers, while I took on bigger tasks. She kept us all running smoothly, stepping in for me when I was too exhausted to correct or re-train our volunteers. Which was exactly what I hired her for!

Above: Our first year woofers hard at work, clearing grass clumps from a freshly broken bed.

Our WWOOFers cleared deadwood, mowed grass, cleared grass clumps from newly plowed beds, and helped me with household tasks. It was far more expensive than I expected (about $2500 for three weeks, due to food and water costs), but the work got done! And a lot of it was very tedious grunt work that I couldn't have possibly taken on while starting seeds, plowing beds, and basically running around like a chicken with my head cut off for 14 hours a day.

As the season continued, my hired hand often became my pinch hitter while I was out frantically foraging or delivering CSAs. Because I had no partner or husband around on a regular basis, she became my second set of hands, as well as a sharp and experienced mind I could bounce business strategies off of. I was lucky to have someone I could trust implicitly, and I will eagerly welcome her back every season she chooses to return. I can honestly say that we wouldn't have gotten half as far as we did without her.

Within the context of a first year farm, with no established routines or processes, it's my opinion that if you really need help, HIRE the most capable and passionate person you can. Research government grants and agricultural initiatives in your area that can help you pay them, and pay them fairly. It is so, so worth it.

Save Your Sanity with Smooth Transactions

Whatever your scale, and whatever your products and services are, you'll be making sales. A sale means a transaction. Ensuring your transactions are painless and convenient for your customers is absolutely essential if you want customers to not only return, but recommend your business to their friends and family.

This starts with having a separate bank account for your business. This key piece makes invoicing, record keeping, and accounting far, far simpler as your business evolves. I cannot stress enough how essential it is to keep your business finances separate from your personal accounts.

Once you have a bank account for your business, you can connect it to Paypal, quickbooks, or your ecommerce website. You can also have customers etransfer funds directly to that account. This is the first step in making your transactions smooth and simple.

Invoices and receipts are the next essential pieces of painless transactions. By using online merchant systems such as Paypal or an ecommerce website, you can very easily create invoices and email them to your customers. Once the invoices are paid, the customers receive automatic receipts, which you will also have access to through your merchant system. This makes finding old transactions very easy, as all records are accessible via a quick search through your merchant system. This of course requires reliable internet, which, like it or not, is a crucial part of doing business in the 21st century.

You can also keep and file hard copy records of each invoice and receipt, but the online merchant systems are a reliable, accessible way to keep them organized.

For my business, I use my website's ecommerce "shop" functions for recurring events like Saturday workshops. I treat the workshops like "items" in my shop, because these workshops happen each Saturday throughout the summer, at the same time every Saturday. I set the dates as "item options", which customers can select, and I limit the "inventory" for each workshop, so I know I'll never have more people sign up than I can accommodate.

For services that require customized bookings, I simply advertise the cost and details of these services, and instruct customers to contact me to book their date and time. From there, I create an invoice through Paypal, and they pay either through the online invoice, or via etransfer. If the customer is local, I will occasionally accept payment by cheque.

For POS (Point Of Sale) transactions at our local markets, we use Square. Again, easy, accessible, affordable, and painless.

At this point, our transactions are seamless, and I rarely encounter any confusion on the customer's end. At the end of my fiscal year, my accountant simply logs into my Paypal, Stripe (via my website), or Square accounts, and has access to all our invoices and receipts. It's so, so easy!

Above: A Square card reader for POS transactions. This photo was taken mid season, as you can see from the state of my hands!

The Erroneous Path of "A Sale is A Sale"

It kills me when I hear of a grower who has put heaps of time and energy into a new product, only to sell a few of them for low prices. But what kills me even more, is hearing "well, a sale is a sale!". No! No it isn't!! A bad sale is a bad sale, and many bad sales will crash your business.

Someone who spends hours creating styled bouquets for their farm stand, then prices them at $15 per bouquet: NO!

Someone who creates intricate stationery with pressed flowers, only to sell them for $3.00 per card: NO!

Someone who spends days or weeks creating holiday wreaths, then sells them for $30 each. NO!

Someone who agrees to supply a small restaurant with centrepieces, but only charges $10 per arrangement. Agh! No!

You could argue they are just trying to compete, or just trying to move their product, but what they're *actually* doing is undercutting themselves AND their product. If all you have to lean on, in terms of marketing, is "cheapest", you will tank your business. Or, you'll lose customers the moment you decide to start charging fair prices.

Low value sales pull in low value customers, and the more you justify them with "a sale is a sale!" the more you'll paint yourself into a corner of bargain hunters, meagre returns, and a dismal cash flow.

Your time and efforts have value. Tell your customers WHY. Take pride in what you do. Focus on your strengths and talents, and showcase them to the world. Don't worry about, or try to emanate, what anyone else is doing. Your situation, your resources, your skills, they're all unique to you alone. Use them!

Maximize your returns by limiting small batch, labour intensive products that can't pull in a profit. Do you know who makes and sells crafts? Hobbyists; people who have other sources of income to lean on (cushion funds for miles!), and lots of time.

You can't compete with hobbyists. If you're here to establish and run a sustainable business, you must think in terms of **input vs. output, cash in vs. cash out**. You should *at least* be including minimum wage into your labour costs. In Alberta, minimum wage is $15/hr. So, if I was to spend 2 hours on a wreath, my labour is worth $30. Add $20 for supplies, and that wreath should cost $50 *minimum*. For myself, I actually value my crafting labour at $35 per hour, because I have a fine art degree, and I'm good at what I do!

The only time it makes sense to justify projects that are labour intensive with low returns, is if they have a specific goal outside of sales. Identify what that goal is before committing to the project, and monitor its success throughout the process of creating and selling it.

A crafty side project could be used to advertise workshops (for said craft), run contests or one-time giveaways, or used as brand building donations. Just remember to clarify that the craft or item is a **one time, exclusive product**. If someone loves it and offers to commission you to create another one, charge them your full, fair price, and go from there.

Creating by commission is a much more efficient way to sell unique crafts and value-added products. When a piece is commissioned, the customer typically understands and appreciates the value of your time and skills. You won't spend hours upon hours building something that you're not sure will even sell. The sale is made first, and then the product is created.

As a small scale grower, and as a very busy farmer, gardener, parent, wife, husband, etc… you can't pretend to be a boutique storefront, with shelves stocked full of darling crafts and products. That's a different business. Stick to your plan, ration your efforts efficiently, and never, *ever* undercut yourself.

Right: pressed Shirley poppies. They don't last long in the vase, but pressing them is easy, and creates potential for off season sales.

Scabisoa "Starflower"

Financials

Deciphering Your Start Up Financials

Financials can be a tad intimidating to anyone new to budgeting or business. From weighing your assets, creating a startup budget, hammering out your projections, finding good bookkeeping software, and identifying funding sources, your financials are really what makes your business a BUSINESS. A lot of people grimace when they think of them, but if you want your business to succeed, it's absolutely critical that you understand them. Once they become familiar, I promise you, they are actually one of the most exciting elements of running a business!

First off, it's very important to mentally differentiate your personal "INCOME" from your business "PROFITS". The two are not the same thing! Your personal income should always be counted as CASH OUT from your business. Those funds are wages that go from your business, to your personal bank account, and must be counted as such. You will obviously need enough money to pay your bills, buy food, and live your life. These are your wages, ie: "personal requirements", and they are an expense to your business, not a profit. If you can cover your personal requirements through other sources of income, then choosing to pay yourself from your business' revenue will depend on whether your cash flow can sustain those wages or not.

When applying for startup loans, if you plan to step into your business as a full-time venture, you MUST include your personal requirements/wages in your CASH OUT projections. These numbers are crucial in identifying gaps in your cash flow, and estimating the correct amount of funds your will require to support your business in its early phase.

Your business' PROFITS are funds that are still a part of the business, they are not a lump of personal spending cash. They are assessed at the end of your fiscal year (usually around tax time). Essentially, if your year-end financial reports show that your business made more than it spent, you will see a profit. Whether that number is $50 or $45000, it's still a profit, and any amount "in the green" is a good thing! Depending on your operating budget, a $50 profit could be considered a small profit, indicating small profit margins, while $45000 could be considered a large profit, showing larger profit margins.

To calculate your profit margins, determine your NET profit (ie: all monies made that year, minus expenses/cash out) and divide it by your GROSS revenue (total monies made that year). So if your business brought in $30000 gross/total in one year, and spent $25000, your net profit will be $5000. Your profit margin will be $5000 ÷ $30 000 = 0.167. To find your margin percentage, multiply the result by 100. In this case, your profit margin would be 16.7%. Not bad!

A business that is financially sustainable should show an operating profit margin of more than 10%, so a 16.7% margin is great! However many businesses won't show a profit at all until their third to fifth year, so remember to BE PATIENT. Hold the course, watch your operating budget, and make carefully weighed financial decisions in your first few years.

It's also important to note that within the first five years of business, it's very likely that all your profits will go straight back into your business to cover infrastructure, equipment, and seeds/bulbs/roots in the following year. Those are your following year's CAPITAL EXPENSES, and will be counted in that following year's budget.

On my website (www.albertagirlacres.com), I've made Five Year Financial Projections spreadsheets available as purchasable downloads. These spreadsheets are designed to help you create your startup budget and work out your five year projections.

The following pages will walk you through how to use those spreadsheets, ensuring they work for YOU:

Instructions

These instructions are short and sweet, but important nonetheless. If you choose not to purchase the Five Year Financial Projections Spreadsheet from my website, these instructions might guide you in creating your own as well.

If you do purchase the spreadsheets, I strongly recommend that you create a working copy of the spreadsheet before beginning, so if anything goes wacky, you'll always have a fresh template to start over with.

Personal Requirements

This is where you'll lay out your personal budget, as well as any additional sources of income, such as a job or spouse's income. If you have a spouse or live-in partner, this is where you'll need to have a very serious conversation about how far their income can carry your dream.

Existing Equipment

Vehicles, tractors, trailers, lawnmowers, rototillers... these are all substantial assets to your growing business. If you already have them, wonderful! They're items that can be spared from your startup budget. If you're applying for funding at any point, potential funders will also want to see this list.

New Equipment

Vehicles, tractors, trailers, lawnmowers, rototillers... if you DON'T have them, they

Below: This is an example of what your early startup equipment expenses might be. Every operation is different, and your early requirements will depend on your budget and resources.

New Equipment			
Item	**Serial #**	**Age**	**Cost**
Tractor & attachments			$9,000.00
Drip irrigation			$3,000.00
Tools & supplies			$1,000.00
Farm truck (used)			$3,500.00
Greenhouse frame (used)	·		$3,500.00
Greenhouse poly			$2,000.00
Cool Bot			$550.00
Air conditioner (used)			$80.00
Horse trailer (used)			$2,500.00
Total Equipment Cost			$25,130.00

Cash Flow Projections - Year 1

Cash In	Start-up	Jan-18	Feb-18	Mar-18	Apr-18
Product Sales		$ -	$ -	$ -	$ -
Accounts Receivable					
Bank/Credit Union/ etc.					
Funding Group					
Personal Investment - Cash					
Other Costs (Start-Up)					
Visa					
Total Cash In (A)	$ -	$ -	$ -	$ -	$ -

Cash Out		Jan-18	Feb-18	Mar-18	Apr-18
Capital Items	$0.00				
Inventory	$0.00				
Renovations	$0.00				
Other Costs (From Start-Up Costs: Business License, Insurance, Website, Supplies & Tools, etc)	$0.00				
Management Wages (Personal Requirements)		$0.00	$0.00	$0.00	$0.00
Loan Payment					
Legal and Accounting					
Vehicle Lease					
Vehicle Expense (Fuel)					
Employee Wages					
WCB					
Marketing					
Membership Fees					
Office Expenses					
Repairs and Maintenance					
Rent/Lease Payment					
Telephone/Internet					
Utilities					
Travel and Entertainment					
Taxes					
Bank Charges					
Miscellaneous					

can be costly. This list will take some research, as you won't want to purchase everything brand new, and you won't NEED every possible piece of equipment right off the bat. Here's what my breakdown looked like (an estimate as we started our year):

Start-Up Costs

Again, these will vary from venture to venture, and my startup expenses will look very different from yours!

An important thing to remember re: first year expenses, is that as you build your business, you'll discover more and more sources for wholesale inventory and supplies. In my first year, I purchased almost all my seeds and bulbs at retail prices. It was expensive!

This is the fun part! Yay projecting sales! Based on the market streams you've identified, your labour capacity, and how much you anticipate producing, you can now get a concrete feel for how those sales could play out.

This worksheet is laid out month by month, and it's important to fill out your anticipated sales as close to when they'll happen as possible. These sales will affect your annual cash flow, which will only project accurately if the sales are entered into their respective months.

Year One

This worksheet could also be titled "GAH!". This is where you'll see your startup budget come into play as it autofills in the green/shaded fields. Complete this worksheet by inputting all of your anticipated overhead and labour expenses, as well as your business's monthly budget.

NOTE: remember you've already created your personal budget, which will automatically be included in this worksheet (yay for the green/shaded fields!), so watch that you don't count certain expenses twice!

Sales Year Two

More fun! Yay for sales!

Year Two

The main difference in your Year Two worksheet is that your startup expenses are no longer included. However, you'll still have annual spring capital expenses like equipment, inventory, or renovations, which you may enter into related fields. I've also made sure to include blank spaces for any additional expenses you may want to include.

Sales Year Three, Year Three, Sales Year Four, Year Four, Sales Year Five, Year Five

When starting up, these years will all be total guesswork, which is why we call them projections! However, lenders will still want to see that you have a carefully considered plan, and laying out five years of financials will help plan and steer your business as the years go on.

Understanding Financial Basics

To start with, it must be made clear that your *Financial Projections* are different from your *Annual Budget*. Within the context of the spreadsheets included on my website, the terms defined below should all have the word "Projected" in front of them.

Capital: This simply means "money" or "funds". "Capital Expenses" or "Capital Items" means annual expenses for equipment and assets.

Overhead: This means the ongoing expense of running a business. In our spreadsheets, your year-to-year "Total Cash Out" is your "Projected Overhead".

Cash Flow: The bottom line of your "Cash Flow Projections", including every field in the "Closing Cash Balance" row, is your Cash Flow, aka your "Projected Cash Flow". It can also be referred to as your "projected bottom line".

The key reason for projections is to identify any gaps in your cash flow, ie: negative amounts. A negative amount in your cash flow, when translated into real life, means no money!

Identifying gaps in your cash flow during the planning process is an opportunity to fix extremely stressful situations before they arrive. Maybe you need to trim your startup expenses, wait to purchase certain items until later in the year, find additional funding (ie: a line of credit), or re-think your market sales streams. In any case, **you cannot show a negative projected cash flow when stepping into your fiscal year.** For one thing, no one will fund you, but also, the MAIN purpose of your business plan is to ensure you aren't sunk six months into your beautiful new business!

Another note about cash flow: If applying for a startup loan through a bank, your projected cash flow is the main thing the bank will look at, aside from loan security. Make it tight!

Gross Revenue: This is your total amount of annual (or your own financial reporting period) sales, prior to any deductions. Within our spreadsheets, this is the number found in your year's end "Total Cash In", in the "TOTAL" column. This is your Projected Gross Revenue.

Net Revenue: This is your total amount of income earned from business operations, minus expenses. Within our spreadsheets, this is the number found in your year end "Closing Cash Balance" in the "TOTAL" column. This is your Projected Net Revenue.

Gross Profit: As confusing as it is, in business, "gross revenue", "gross profit", and "net profit" are very different things. "Gross profit" refers to net revenue minus cost of sales. This term may come into play once you're creating your annual budgets, but for the purposes of your projections, it's simpler to just include cost of sales in your overhead, and use "Net Profit" to determine your business' profits.

Net Profit: This refers to deducting cost of sales from your net revenue. You'll find your year end projected Net Profit in December's "Closing Cash Balance".

That's as deep as we'll get into business terminology for now. As your business grows and becomes established, more of these terms will come up, and will become more familiar to your venture. For now, focus on the basics!

Once you have your first year of operations established, it will be necessary for you to create an Annual Budget based on your year-end income statements, balance sheets, and cash flow reports. All of these financial elements can be created and maintained in bookkeeping software such as Quickbooks, Freshbooks, Sage 50cloud, Xero, and others. Alberta Girl Acres uses Quickbooks, and I find it fairly easy to learn and navigate. Quickbooks also offers several free courses, webinars, and tutorials. For feedback and reviews on other options, it's often helpful to reach out to your personal networks.

Personally, I LOVE playing with financial projections. They've become my go-to every time I have a new idea and want to see how it could play into our year's revenue. If want to have a bit of ridiculous fun, I'll plug in some REALLY optimistic (ie: impossible) sales projections and just daydream about my astronomically successful (but very hypothetical) business. Then I'll come back to earth and plug the far more moderate, realistic numbers in. One can dream!

Once you've learned how to use the projections worksheets, they become a bit magical, like a crystal ball for your business. Of course, they're still just projections, and there's still a TON of work involved in turning those projections into reality, but I still find them extremely exciting!

Loans

Due to our short growing season, a strong, wind resistant greenhouse frame was an essential startup purchase for my farm.

"You'll need a tractor"

When I first started letting my little world know that I was starting a flower farm, I can't tell you how many people found it pertinent to tell me, "well, you'll need a tractor". To this day, I still don't understand what they thought my plan was, if they were assuming I hadn't even thought of a *tractor* yet.

Yes, you'll need a tractor. But tractors are VERY expensive, so approach this startup cost thoughtfully.

In your first year, you'll be breaking a lot of ground, which will require a heavy duty piece of equipment (aka: a tractor!). But once those beds are dug and amended, you can actually get by quite comfortably without a giant rumbling machine, and the massive upfront expense of one might not justify itself as it sits quietly, relatively unused for the rest of the season.

In Jean-Martin Fortier's The Market Gardener, he covers low till/no till growing methods extensively, detailing the benefits of soil building and minimal tillage, all while using the humble, smaller, and much less expensive walk-behind tractor.

Not to be confused with a garden rototiller, a walk-behind tractor is still a heavy duty machine! For small scale operations, its various attachments can break ground, spread compost, cultivate beds, and perform a vast range of other market farm tasks. The main difference between it and a conventional small tractor, is it demands much more from your body, in terms of maneuvering. If you enjoy physical exercise, this isn't a problem. I'm 5'2", 125lbs, and can handle our BCS 732 just fine. It's a workout, to be sure, but certainly not outside my physical capacity.

In terms of startup expenses, a walk-behind tractor makes much more economic sense. A new walk-behind BCS tractor with a rotary plow attachment is less than $10k, compared to a small conventional tractor that would start at $50k, at least.

If you have more room in your budget and are aiming to grow on more than one acre, perhaps leasing a small Kubota or a similar tractor would make more sense than buying one outright. Especially in your early years, when your customer base hasn't yet been established and cash flow is tight.

And of course, if you have friendly farmer neighbours, get to know them and ask if they would be willing to break ground on your new beds. Then do the less intensive work, like amendments, using your walk-behind.

So YES, you'll need a tractor, but you don't have to buy a $100k machine in your first year! Your main tasks early on will be breaking ground in the fall or spring, and then minimal tilling/plowing, amendments, and weeding. By the end of your first couple of years, you'll have a much better sense of what sort of major equipment you'll actually need, and you'll have a steadier cash flow to justify those purchases.

In our first year, we broke about 1/4 acre of beds using my dear little BSC 732. In our second year, our farmer neighbours helped break our field with their tractor, and I used the BCS to create furrowed rows. I still use the BSC often, and absolutely love it.

FINDING FUNDING

If you decide to seek startup loans, there are several programs and organizations out there that can help. And then of course, there's the bank! Or your family?

One thing you will absolutely need before approaching funders is a detailed business plan, as well as five year projections showing a balanced cash flow. Government lending organizations will want to see the business plan first, banks will want to see the projections first.

Every province, state, and country has different resources for business loans. To find lending bodies in your area, ask other small scale growers, search government websites, and research online.

Grants

Grants are government or corporate funds created through private, national, provincial, or state-wide programs for the specific purpose of supporting and growing local economies.

Be wary while researching and applying for grants. While larger corporation initiatives are ususally legitimate (ie: FedEx Small Business Grants, Enmax Community Outreach, etc), there are many false offerings out there as well. Remember that if something seems too good to be true, it probably is. The last thing you want to do is tangle your finances with a high interest scam.

Government grants are by far the safest and most legitimate sources to apply for funding, but they certainly aren't easy money. Writing a grant takes much more time than simply submitting an application, and extensive proof of your business' legitimacy will be required in the process. This means your business must be at least registered as a trade, and some programs only accept businesses that have been in operation for at least one taxable year.

That said, if you're willing to do some hunting and fill out a bit of paperwork, there are definitely funds out there that could significantly boost your new business.

In America, the primary resource for small

farm grants is the United States Department of Agriculture (USDA), and operating as an extension, the National Resources Conservation Service (NRCS) offers several programs as well.

In Canada, the federal government offers several funding programs for a variety of small business and agricultural needs. For small farms, the most useful resource is Agriculture and Agri-Food Canada. In their programs and services, they list several funding initiatives. One that was particularly useful to us in our first year was the Agricultural Youth Green Jobs Initiative, supported through their Youth In Agriculture stream. The grant we recieved from that program supplemented 1/3 of our farm hand's income in that first year.

It's also worthwhile to check out the Government of Canada's Wage Subsidies and Other Assistance Programs for small businesses. Remember, you're a small business too! There are many summer employee subsidy programs that could be useful to you.

Each Canadian province also has Canadian Agricultural Partnership programs that help fund projects such as "Farm Water Supply" and "Irrigation Efficiency".

It's also worthwhile to investigate local community-focused funding bodies in your area. These are often government-funded organizations designed to build community, and many offer small grants for worthwhile projects.

While government grants are excellent resources for new farmers, they aren't "free money". Many are subsidiary grants, meaning they will reimburse up to one third or one half of the funds for the project you received the grant for. So, if your project costs, $15 000, the grant may only cover $5000. They also require detailed reports before disbursal, which may include pay stubs and bank records.

The process of receiving a government grant usually goes: 1) Apply, 2) Grant is accepted (hopefully!), 3) Your season commences, and you keep detailed records, 4) Season ends, report is submitted, 5) DIdisbursal of funds. Note that the funds typically come at the *end* of the season. You will still need enough revenue to balance your cash flow, without the grant, throughout the season.

Of course, I'm speaking from my experience with Canadian grants. Different countries and states could very well have different processes. Just be sure to clarify what those processes are before counting on early season grant funds.

Now What?

So you have a plan, now what?

REGISTRATION

There are several excellent resources that take you through the business registration process step by step. For Canadians, the best place to start is the Government of Canada's website, at https://canadabusiness.ca/government/registering-your-business. There, they walk you through the different types of business, ie: sole proprietorship, partnership, corporation, and co-operative.

For new growers in other countries, a quick google search such as "business registration [your country]" should guide to you relevant government websites. Your government's website is the FIRST place you should look for such information, as it will be the most accurate and legitimate.

In your first year of business, the simplest way to get started is as a sole proprietor. If you have a partner, then obviously a partnership makes more sense. In Canada it's very easy to register as a sole proprietor. Again, search your respective government's websites for information on registering your business.

In Canada/Alberta, if you anticipate grossing less than $30,000 in your first year, you also won't need a GST/HST tax account, and likewise you won't have to register with the CRA (Canada Revenue Agency), and if you won't have staff on payroll, you won't need a WCB account (Worker's Compensation Board). These rules may be different in other countries however, so be sure to look into all the requirements for your area before opening for business.

"Do I HAVE to register?"

In Canada, entrepreneurs may do business under their given names (ie: Laura Smith) without having to register their trade name, however the moment you add ANY other word to your name (ie: Laura Smith Flowers), whether on invoices, in your web profiles, or any marketing, you become susceptible to fines for not having a registered trade name.

You've come this far, and if you are indeed serious about launching a cut flower business, registering your trade name is an integral part of that. Not only does it create a degree of separation between you and your business, but it also legitimizes you in the eyes of banks, clients, and potential funders. Registering also gives you access to many wholesalers who only sell to registered businesses.

If you're planning to do a "trial year", it might make sense to simply operate under your given name and sell only to friends and family. However, if you plan to advertise, market, and seek interest from the general public, you should definitely register a trade name.

LICENSING AND PERMITS

Depending where you're located and how you plan to sell, licences and permits may vary. My farm is zoned as "General Use", and therefore a business licence was not required. However, if I were to sell my product in any nearby towns/cities (separate from a farmer's market),

I would likely require a business licence for each respective city or town.

Many farmer's markets provide umbrella business licensing to their vendors, so if your farm doesn't otherwise require a business license, and the only place you're selling flowers is a farmers market, be sure to confirm they have vendor business licensing covered.

Because every farm and business is so different, the best way to find out exactly what you'll need regarding licensing and permits is to call your city or county directly and ask them. They are often very friendly and more than happy to point you in the right direction.

INSURANCE

Most farms require Commercial General Liability insurance or Farm Liability Insurance, which primarily covers equipment and protects them from liability if someone is injured on their farm. Some funding groups will also require that you have life insurance, and will request being added to your insurance in the event of catastrophe (they want their money back either way).

Again, the type of insurance you'll require will depend very much on where you are, and what your business entails. Many farmer's markets require that you have insurance, and will require proof before approving your participation.

Once you have a business plan, complete with a better sense of what you'll be doing, call an insurance broker and ask for advice and quotes on what types of insurance will be required.

BENEFITS

As a new small business owner, accessing health benefits can be a serious "make or break" consideration before choosing to fly solo as an independent business. If you don't have a partner or spouse with benefits, if your federal government doesn't offer any form of health care, or if your government's care doesn't cover dental, mental health, and prescriptions, you may be eligible for reduced rate group benefits from various sources. Insurance companies, local chambers of commerce, farm bureaus, Christian ministries, and casual part time work are all possible options for health insurance.

Certainly, in addition to securing health benefits, ensuring your business is SAFE in terms of proper chemical and equipment usage is paramount when running a market farm or garden. Avoid risking unnecessary illness or accident, especially if you have a limited health safety net!

Below: Fall flower bulbs.

Bare peony roots were another "essential" startup purchase for me. Peonies take at least three years until they can be harvested, so start them as early as you can!

Resources & Research

One note before we step into this chapter:

Many of us are trained, either by our previous work experiences or by societal conditioning, to "wait for permission". We feel we aren't "allowed" to do something until a more experienced authority gives us the green light.

In my experience, "research" can sometimes enable this conditioning, making us believe we can't, or shouldn't, step forward until we have every piece of information we can find, from every expert we can glean from. We wait for approval. We hold off, telling ourselves we're being prudent, when really we're simply too afraid to make the jump.

Learning can be exhilarating, but it can also be extremely uncomfortable. It can be downright scary.

While starting a business is no small thing, and research is absolutely critical to starting it as wisely as possible, launching your venture will also require immense amounts of bravery.

You don't *need* a horticultural degree to start a flower farm. You don't *need* a business degree either. You don't need to buy memberships to grower's associations and societies, and you don't need to attend expensive annual conferences to legitimize yourself as a grower or businessperson. You should have SOME growing experience (ideally a gardening obsession you've finally decided to let consume your entire life), but you don't need to be a "pro" to get started.

Really, the only way to become a cut flower farmer, is to BE a cut flower farmer. Develop YOUR business YOUR way. Experiment. Learn about plants and soil. Don't wait for permission, and don't wait for others to legitimize you. Simply DO. Once you are DOING, those connections, memberships, and networks will emerge naturally, according to YOUR business needs and YOUR vision.

I've created a list of some great places to learn more about growing cut flowers, gardening for market, and connecting with others in the industry. This list is by no means complete, and you'll find each resource will open up another world of further references and reading!

ONLINE

Association of Specialty Cut Flower Growers (International): www.ascfg.org. "The ASCFG was created to educate, unite, and support commercial cut flower growers. It does this by providing production and marketing information; connecting members through events and communications; supporting floriculture research; and encouraging the purchase and use of locally grown flowers by the public. Its mission is to help growers produce high-quality floral material, and to foster and promote the local availability of that product."

Australian Flower Council (Australia): www.australianflowercouncil.org.au. "Established to encourage unity and communication within the flower industry. It is intended that membership will consist of growers, wholesalers and florists who are dedicated in ensuring the continued prosperity and development of the flower industry."

The British Flower Collective (Great Britain): www.thebritishflowercollective.com. "Working together to put "seasonality", "local" and "British" back into the flower industry"

Floret Farm: www.floretflowers.com. Erin Benzakein's blogs, tutorials, and mini workshops are bliss! And of course, her online cut flower growing course and her book, Cut Flower Garden are wonderful resources.

Flowers Australia (Australia): www.flowersaustralia.org. "Flowers Australia represents growers,

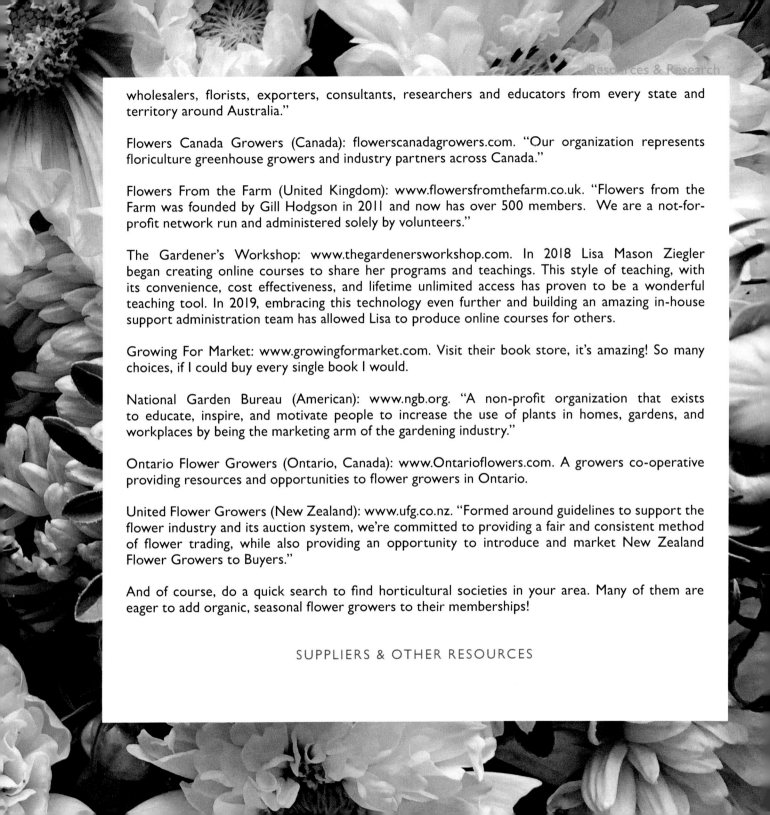

wholesalers, florists, exporters, consultants, researchers and educators from every state and territory around Australia."

Flowers Canada Growers (Canada): flowerscanadagrowers.com. "Our organization represents floriculture greenhouse growers and industry partners across Canada."

Flowers From the Farm (United Kingdom): www.flowersfromthefarm.co.uk. "Flowers from the Farm was founded by Gill Hodgson in 2011 and now has over 500 members. We are a not-for-profit network run and administered solely by volunteers."

The Gardener's Workshop: www.thegardenersworkshop.com. In 2018 Lisa Mason Ziegler began creating online courses to share her programs and teachings. This style of teaching, with its convenience, cost effectiveness, and lifetime unlimited access has proven to be a wonderful teaching tool. In 2019, embracing this technology even further and building an amazing in-house support administration team has allowed Lisa to produce online courses for others.

Growing For Market: www.growingformarket.com. Visit their book store, it's amazing! So many choices, if I could buy every single book I would.

National Garden Bureau (American): www.ngb.org. "A non-profit organization that exists to educate, inspire, and motivate people to increase the use of plants in homes, gardens, and workplaces by being the marketing arm of the gardening industry."

Ontario Flower Growers (Ontario, Canada): www.Ontarioflowers.com. A growers co-operative providing resources and opportunities to flower growers in Ontario.

United Flower Growers (New Zealand): www.ufg.co.nz. "Formed around guidelines to support the flower industry and its auction system, we're committed to providing a fair and consistent method of flower trading, while also providing an opportunity to introduce and market New Zealand Flower Growers to Buyers."

And of course, do a quick search to find horticultural societies in your area. Many of them are eager to add organic, seasonal flower growers to their memberships!

SUPPLIERS & OTHER RESOURCES

Seeds

- Baker Creek Heirloom Seeds (International)
- Chiltern Seeds (UK, International)
- Dutch Garden Seeds (Holland, UK)
- Eden Brothers (US)
- Edgebrook Farm (Canada)
- Floret (US, Canada, European Union, UK, Switzerland, Iceland, Australia)
- GEO Seeds (International)
- Harris Seeds (US)
- Hawthorn Farm Organic Seeds (Canada)
- Johnny's Selected Seeds (International)
- Magic Garden Seeds (Europe)
- Swallowtail Garden Seeds (International)
- Thompson & Morgan Wholesale (UK)
- Vitalis Organic Seeds (Europe)
- West Coast Seeds (North America)
- Whistling Prairie Flowers (Canada)
- William Dam Seeds (Canada)
- Wild About Flowers (Wildflowers, Canada)
- Zollinger Seeds (Switzerland, Europe)
- Gardenseeds.org, a list of organic seed suppliers throughout Europe

Bulbs, Plugs, Roots, Plants

- A.D.R. Bulbs (North America)
- Creekside Growers - dahlias and peonies (Canada)
- Creek Hill Nursery (US)
- Connie's Dahlias (Canada)
- Botanus (North America)
- Burnaby Lake Greenhouses (BC, Western Canada)
- De Groot (US)
- De Vroomen (Canada)
- Edgebrook Farm (Canada)
- Eurobulb (Europe)
- Farmer Bailey (US)
- Fred C. Gloekner & Company Inc (International)
- Gro N Sell (plugs, US)
- Growing Colors (US)
- Heirloom Roses (US)

- Italian Ranunculus (US)
- Jolly Farmer (plugs, Canada, North America)
- K. van Bourondien & Sons (Europe)
- Lakeshore WIllows (Canada)
- Norseco (plugs, Canada)
- Parker's Wholesale (UK)
- Peter Nyssen (Europe)
- Stone Meadow Gardens (Canada)
- Swedish Touch Peonies (North America)
- Unicorn Blooms (Canada)
- Van Noort (International)
- Whistling Prairie Flowers (Canada)

Wholesale Supplies
- Amazon (International)
- AM Leonard (US)
- Dutch Garden Supplies (Europe)
- Floralife (US)
- Florists Supply Ltd (Canada)
- Folia (Europe)
- Garden Centre Fresh (Europe)
- Garden Supply Direct (Europe)
- Global Horticultural (Canada)
- HJS Wholesale (Canada)
- Horticentre (New Zealand)
- Pioneer Gardens (North America)
- The Professional Gardener (Alberta, Canada)
- ULINE (North America)
- United Farmers of Alberta Co-operative Ltd, UFA (Alberta)
- Van Horn (US)

Other Resource Tips
- Safeway gives away used black buckets if you're nice to them! (North America)
- Kijiji and Craigslist are great places to find used supplies and equipment
- Check out agricultural auctions in your area for deals on equipment and infrastructure (ie: greenhouses)
- Make friends with your farmer neighbours!

Deep Breath, Jump In...

"Let us not forget that the cultivation of the earth is the most important labor of man. When tillage begins, other arts will follow. The farmers, therefore, are the founders of civilization." - Daniel Webster

I wish you the very best, whether you're dreaming, obsessively planning, or already knees-deep in your cut flower business. This is a beautiful, challenging, and incredibly satisfying world to be a part of. I hope this book has helped you visualize your future in cut flower farming, and I look forward to crossing paths with many new growers in the coming seasons.

And if you enjoyed this book, or found it useful for your business visioning and development, please post a review online, and share it with your friends!

Many thanks and happy planning,

Sarah

Made in the USA
Monee, IL
29 November 2021

83391474R00126